KFAR SAMA: A VILLAGE IN LEBANON

MANSOUR LABAKY

Kfar Sama

A Village in Lebanon

Translated by Erasmo Leiva-Merikakis

IGNATIUS PRESS   SAN FRANCISCO

Title of the French original:
Kfar Sama
published in Lebanon by Editions Al-Karmah

Second edition co-published by Editions Al-Karmah (Lebanon) and
Téqui (Paris) under the title:
Kfar Sama, Village du Liban: Pourquoi la guerre?

Contents

Foreword

I once lived in Lebanon, and the impression I took away from this country was one of *joyfulness*. I would then recite to myself Péguy's verses on the first days of creation, from his poem *Eve*:

And God, Himself at once young and eternal,
Contemplated the bloom of the flower of young age;
And, as Father, He looked with a father's regard
On the world, humbly gathered up like a village.

And what I now see on the television screen is this same Lebanon ravaged, massacred, torn to shreds, a theater of violence and chaos. Previously I had been present at the beginning of the world. I now have the feeling of assisting at the end of the world, as if the drama of history, of creation, of the Passion, of the Resurrection were being acted out in abridged form in this beloved land.

I was turning over these somber thoughts when I received the kind visit of Father Mansour Labaky, who came to give me a copy of *Kfar Sama*.[1]

This is a truly admirable book, and one difficult to define. Like Pascal's *Pensées* it is written with blood and tears. More than a book it is really a cry of the heart. . . .

In his heart, which this war has pierced with a sword, he unites the two distinct vocations of priest and poet. His language is made up of fire and light, and without transition he can pass, like Job or Jeremiah, from indignation to adoration.

[1] Arabic for "Village of Heaven".

We Occidentals [original: "we French"], who have been spared these unspeakable trials, cannot read these pages without a feeling of deep pity. How can we help our Lebanese brothers? If we could only realize how much we suffer from our remoteness from them, from our dire impotence. The sacrifice of our soldiers is the symbol of our compassion.

But what most greatly struck me in this book full of sorrows is the truth that Lebanon is a land of "hope against hope", a promise of resurrection. What in this poem comes to triumph over suffering, what bursts out from each page of this hymn to joy through pain, is precisely *joyfulness*, the spirit of childhood, the certainty of the dawn. And so, in the end, I again see my first impression of Lebanon confirmed: Lebanon land of *joyfulness*. Salvation will yet again come to us from the East.

Jean Guitton
of the Académie Française

Part One

The Village

ONCE UPON A TIME there was a little Lebanese village, nestled in the wooded flank of a marvelous mountain.

It was born one evening (or was it a morning?), now buried in long-past ages, no one could say just when.

Lady Nature, invited to its baptism, brought it landscapes as presents: the sea and a multitude of mountains undulating as far as the eye can see.

Into its bassinet of green she also poured houses with archways, with a headdress of red tiles; an air purer than a caliph's diamonds; also enchanted waterfalls, birds and flowers.

In a word, nothing but very old-fashioned things. . . .

And, finally, she called it Kfar Sama; only Heaven knows why.

This little village grew in age and wisdom. From the moment it started babbling, it took to living peaceful days, cadenced by work, prayer and song.

Like all happy people, it had no history.

And yet. . .

Its summers were still fragrant like springs; its winters wore the reddish browns of autumn, brightening up the pines' green

A multitude of mountains undulating far as the eye can see

tufts with shades of gold and russet. Sometimes it even snowed, if such was the whim of the winds, which plucked at the clouds for the children's delight.

Oh, how good life was, and deep, and fecund, in this little Lebanese village nestled in the wooded flank of a marvelous mountain!

⚜

The inhabitants of Kfar Sama were gentle and humble of heart, slow to anger, quick to be reconciled.

Also, they radiated friendship and hospitality; they were naturally talkative, curious, hard-working, frugal, honest, and given to boasting.

They helped one another and shared what they had, and together they sang and danced their native songs and dances; they revelled in the *zajal*[1] and in backgammon, and they practiced many crafts and grew vegetables and fruits.

They loved the smell of the earth after the first autumn rain, and the sunsets that tinged the horizon with purple, and the fruit that could be plucked from the branches, and all the splendors that God had given them as their inheritance.

With rare exceptions (and these no doubt were there to confirm the rule), they knew nothing of ambition, insomnia or hatred.

⚜

[1] A poetic contest in dialect. It is improvised, sung in rhyme and rhythm, and takes place between two or more contestants. In Lebanon the *zajal* is the most important form of popular poetry.

Houses with archways

These good country folk had strange customs.

Listen!

At table they always kept one place free. This, they said, was for the friend, the relative, the poor man, or just any passer-by who would cross their threshold at meal time. In this way he would know that he was expected and that he was far from "falling like a hair in the soup"; his place was already prepared and his presence welcome.

And there is more.

At night a lamp was keeping watch at the entrance to each house.

For quite some time now the city-folk, drowned in their urban noises, and the rich, bristling with privileges and numbers, have been unable to hear the irrational language of these out-moded lights.

This is what they said:

"My house is your house, O brother that passes by in the night. If you are weary, if you are hungry, if you need help or friends, come in and be welcome."

Truly, truly they were strange, these people of past times, naive and old-fashioned as their landscapes.

And yet. . .

They had nothing against progress.

At Kfar Sama the arrival of running water and electricity (long, long after they had arrived in the main cities and villages of the country, and after the atom bomb had been invented overseas) was the occasion of memorable celebrations. People danced until very late in the village square, to the accompaniment of the *oud*,[2] the *derbaké*[3] and the *nay*.[4] The *zajal* released its flows of poetry, and, in the general euphoria, the frogs in the brooks croaked blissfully to the rhythm of the tambourines.

As for motorcars, they did not shove the donkeys aside, far from it! Quite simply, Kfar Sama appreciated with much dignity—and a pinch of ecstasy—the innumerable services they offered, coughing all the while.

Shouey, shouey,[5] various sorts of machines crept into the rhythms of the village. They modified certain ways of doing work, but not at all the character of the people.

Machines, it's well known, tend to gobble up man and nature alike. But it's also well known that mountain folk have roots that sink to the very heart of the earth. It takes time, patience and tons of cunning to get the better of them.

And thus, whether by donkey or by car, Kfar Sama moved on at its own unhurried pace, with its nose to the wind from the mountaintops and its soul to God's hidden springs.

Listen still!

Sure as the sun shines on the world, God lived with these people.

[2] Arabian lute.
[3] Arabian drum that is struck, in alternation, with the palms and the fingers of both hands.
[4] Oriental wooden flute.
[5] Little by little.

With their addiction to fresh air and open doors, you see, and the childlike candor of their ways of relating, God did not have to knock or give any password in order to be let into their houses.

The poet says: "As long as a reed remains closed it can receive no secrets, nor can it resound in response to lip and breath."

And our friends hold: "As long as a man shuts his heart and his house, he remains a stranger to his brothers and cannot claim to welcome God."

And so year in and year out the seasons continued to spin the thread of time, and every dawn sang the eternity of these people who, simply because they loved, felt their life solidly beneath them.

When War arrived, Kfar Sama had a hard time accepting its existence. War was beyond its grasp.

Kfar Sama rejected it with all its soul, with all its prayers and with all its tears. And when its houses were destroyed and most of its townsfolk mowed down, it understood that tears and outrage did not have the least chance of appeasing the folly of men.

It understood that now it had to love as much and even more than before; it had to give as much and even more, so that love and self-giving might flood the earth in an ocean of light.

Because it's when we stop loving that the darkness of death begins.

WAR RUMBLED one April morning, just as the Easter bells were beating their wings and the buttercups were beginning to dot the prairies.

From what burnt-out sphere, from what secret promises did War thus bound forth with its plumage of flames, riding a black stallion with flanks teeming with threats?

Won't its mad patrol ever come to an end?

From East to West, from the virgin forests to the farthest island, War rides on and on and on, and it seizes the riches of the earth, and it seizes the riches of man, and it turns them into the tools of death.

And men plunge into War's dark arenas, and they become burnt-out souls, bodies broken in its bloody jousts, and they run, run, run . . . this people attacking that people, brothers attacking brothers.

And yet! The same God is in Heaven, the same Heaven is there for the whole earth, and myriads of stars shine for the infiniteness of each human being!

It rumbled one April morning. . . .

O bells of Easter, Redemption and Resurrection! Immaculate lambs on fresh pastures! Clusters of trees and little golden chicks, fluffy and gentle as the smile of a child!

"Blessed are the gentle, for the earth will be theirs."

"Blessed are the peacemakers, for Heaven itself will be theirs."

It rumbled one April morning. . . .

What did War want from tiny Lebanon, green and blue like a dragonfly, when in the fields the dew was distilling honey from the clover? Did it want her springs of water? Or her thousand suns, bigger than her mauve-blue sky? Or her rains, that quench her dreams of harvest?

What does it want; for what does it search, going from one end of the earth to the other? The death of all dawns under skies that have crumbled? Or the death of all men in an abyss of darkness?

"When God began creating heaven and earth, the earth was deserted and void, and darkness was on the surface of the abyss. God separated the light from the darkness. There was an evening, there was a morning."

It rumbled one April morning!

The light once again joined the darkness. There was no more evening, there was no more morning. And in the night the lamps lost their reason for being, and the wide-open doors wailed when struck by unfamiliar bolts.

And God covered His face!

Those who knew, those who awaited it, gave War a queen's welcome. Their hearts long since closed off, they hastened to throw open the gates of Hell's arsenals.

All the others, along with God, covered their faces.

But in their starless night they lighted God's own lamps: their oil was communion, prayers, songs, tears.

Beyond the chaos, beyond all wars, these lamps glow softly like soft eternal dawns. They have eyes like children's and voices like mothers'. They let in suffering and they let in death and they create a sky dappled with tenderness for all those who are lost in a night without name.

They are there, these lamps! It's enough to open up your heart, to say No to hatred, and you'll float with them over the seven oceans, where the dead are no longer afraid because they *know* they're alive.

ONLY YESTERDAY. . . .

It was six o'clock, the hour of Aïn el-Farah.[6]

With jars perched on their shoulders, the women of Kfar Sama filed one by one by the spring.

They told each other a thousand little stories, which had already been recounted a thousand times and listened to a thousand times, and always with the same interest and the same exclamations of approval or reproach.

It was their life which they thus emptied out in the evening breeze, at the same time as they filled their jars.

To quench one's thirst, to dilute the syrups gotten from different berries, from cherries, oranges or sweet-lemons, to drown the *arak*[7] in tiny, finely chiselled glasses, nothing was like pure spring water.

"Drink in gladness and peace, O my brother, my father, my child, my sister, my husband.

"Drink in gladness and peace, O unknown brother who honors our roof with your trusting presence.

"These are the berries from our garden, and the water from Aïn el-Farah.

[6] Well of Happiness.
[7] National drink, made from fermented grape juice and anise.

"It comes into the light in the little grove of plane trees and poplars where the mountain hollows out to provide it with a festal path.

"It comes from the heart of the earth.

"Drink with your soul as well as with your mouth, O my brother, because this water draws on the earth and the sky, draws on the rustling of the poplars and the song of the birds and the crystalline purity of God's love.

"See how fresh and transparent it is! I drew it at the hour when the shepherd's star presides over the sunset.

"See how pure and fresh it is! May it purify your soul with the happiness, the peace and the prosperity of the humble!"

Only yesterday. . . .

This is how the women of Kfar Sama used to speak, because they had always known that to offer water from the spring was to offer Life.

⚜

Life: they knew its weight and its inestimable worth.

Up at the crack of dawn, day after day they were busy weaving the well-being of their little world.

Whether exhausted or full of zest, they washed, cooked, prepared preserves according to the season, patched clothes, nursed their babies, rocked them to sleep, comforted the sick, and prayed—without ever a complaint.

They knew they held the lamps of their homes between their fecund hands, and they venerated them as they would monstrances.

The peace and sturdy health of their households were their most precious possession. And their patience and their indulgence had all the majestic opulence of a river irrigating a plain.

They were all at once ciborium, cradle and wheatfield, as they—along with Mary, in the silence where promises germinate —knew how to embrace both God and the world in one and the same glance.

⚜

Life: they knew its sweet weight and its incomparable light.

They heard it with awe-struck certainty in the first cries of their newborn.

Who can speak of death at the birth of a little human being?

Who can speak of the void at the blossoming of a smile?

Who can speak of the absurdity of life when a mother is nursing her child?

When someone is giving a portion of her very self?

Who can speak of war when, following their mothers, the children carry jugs to the Well of Happiness and take long drinks, while bathed in living water, laughs and tenderness?

⚜

Only yesterday. . . .

They were happy!

They still knew nothing of the cruelty of those who are not afraid to inflict death.

The children carry jugs and take long drinks.

With their mothers they believed that all men were their brothers.

With their fathers they believed that, since man was animated by the breath of God, "everything he pointed to was to bear the name of 'living being' ".

Their world was big, as big as Kfar Sama, with the sea at its feet and its forehead in the clouds.

Their laughs were pearly, pearly like Kfar Sama, with its cascades of exuberant affection.

Their games were rich, rich like Kfar Sama, with the inexhaustible treasures of its thick woods and their mysterious caves, full of whispers.

Their prayers were fervent, fervent like Kfar Sama, which drew its offerings from the wellspring of its people's hearts.

Only yesterday. . . .

They were happy, in natural harmony with the peace that is God's.

And the hour of Aïn el-Farah would idle on, light and rustling like an apricot tree in bloom.

Today. . . .

Happiness began to float in suspension, strangely unreal and immobile, as if detained at the edge of an inescapable chasm.

And the children discovered, along with fear, how incredibly easy it is to kill a soul and its ability to love eternally once the night of hatred has destroyed the sun in that soul.

⚜

Only yesterday. . . .

The men of Kfar Sama saw that the bread won by the sweat of their brows—in joy and in sorrow, in the sereneness of the mountains and in the gratitude of their hearts—had the aroma of a prayer when it nourished their children.

And death, at the end of the road, belonged to the order of life. Because man, just like the seed, had to return to the earth in order to soar up to the light.

And that was good!

Tomorrow. . . .

Will there be any tomorrows for nations intoxicated with mechanisms of death that they produce as on an assembly line?

Will there be any tomorrows for the supermen of today, who push their shamelessness to the point of putting arms into the hands of children, knowingly and systematically?

Will there be any tomorrows for men who mow down men and their own souls, because they no longer believe that to kill is to die twice over, once to the earth and once to the infinite light?

"Rabbi, what must I do to inherit eternal life?"

"Thou shalt love thy God with all thy heart, with all thy soul and with all thy mind, and thy neighbor as thyself.

"Do this and thou wilt have life."

Yesterday, today, tomorrow. . . . You receive the earth and the sky as your inheritance. And behold that from East to West, from the virgin forests to the farthest island, "the voice of your brother's blood cries up to Me from the ground. What have you done with him?"

"Nothing, Rabbi! It's not my fault! What can I do if the world sows hatred and harvests weapons? What can I do if each of our steps seems to set off a massacre?"

⚜

Yesterday, today, tomorrow. . . . The souls of Kfar Sama pray with all the gentle souls on earth:

"Rabbi, You have given us life so that we can create in Your image and make the stuff of life emerge from the earth.

"You have given us hands that we may fill them and open them to everyone we encounter, and not to reduce living beings and landscapes into shreds of desolation.

"You have placed Your peace and Your goodness between our hands. Do not let us forget it!"

Part Two

Jeddo

S TORIES ARE ENTHRALLING when their first words portend that in the end paradise will be regained. "Once upon a time there was a village . . . a house . . . a people . . . who for a long time lived in peace and happiness."

That is how the story of Kfar Sama begins. But storms coming from elsewhere deprived it of its cloudless conclusion.

Its conclusion? Far from it! Even as I speak to you, this village in ruins has not broken the thread of its story. Because if love has neither beginning nor end, neither could a story of Life ever end.

So listen on!

Evening is falling: an evening full of the hues of springtime. It's the eighth spring since War arrived in our country. The third since the destruction of Kfar Sama. And War still does not let off. It gnaws and gnaws, looking for some still untouched parcels of land. It is madly indifferent to time, whose task it becomes to increase sufferings. It is madly indifferent to day or night. It is madly indifferent to the marvelling laughter of a child that discovers the first violets. It knows nothing of hours or seasons or prayers. It only knows of burnt lands. And death.

Spring!

Once again the earth awakens from its long winter sleep. Life is born again on the plains; softly it climbs up the mountains, and the white summits shimmer with gold and silver at the sunrise. Soon they will take off their ermine mantle and again put on their tunics with the colors of the rainbow.

Spring!

What about the spring of men? What becomes of their wars in the pure breeze of this general rebirth?

Everywhere the flowers open their petals, shimmering with the blue of the sky, the pufflike clouds and strings of dewdrops. Everywhere the streams hum their barcarolles, and the ploughing shapes the fields into so many patens for the harvest.

Everywhere there is life! In radiances, fragrances, symphonies. After its rest the earth now receives the seed, and what War scatters is death, death, and more death.

What about the spring of men?

⚜

So many things are said to justify wars.

So many things are said to justify its sufferings and miseries.

So many things are said . . . that become the creed of a frightened and frightening world.

But what man's reason wants to believe is often unacceptable to man's heart, especially to the simple hearts which know nothing of the swaying interests that arbitrarily cut up the earth.

Kfar Sama, for one, functioned much too little at the level of these speculations to admit the merit of any war whatever. With so many other little villages on earth, naive and old-fashioned like their landscapes, Kfar Sama kept a child's heart which beat at the rhythm of its faith, of its tenderness, and of nature; a heart which had the patience of winters that hold seeds and the heat of summers that ripen promises. This is why, in spite of the earth's atmosphere, so dense in conflicts, so opaque with injustices that it succeeds in masking Heaven from us, Kfar Sama continued to reach out to Heaven through its love and its respect for all things.

⚜

Children of Lebanon: you know that not long ago there still existed Kfar Samas by the handful in our mountains. I do not mean they represent the very model of happiness. But my claim is that the Kingdom of God is to be found in every community where each person is loved and respected for himself; where every newcomer is welcomed as a brother; where the differences, far from making for competition, become a complementarity at the service of all. And in this Kingdom it is impossible ever to come to understand how men could be set up to kill one another. Such a project could never be explained, whether by reason, the heart or by appeal to fate.

For all its naivete, Kfar Sama was aware that War is a defeat in itself, an abdication of the Spirit in us.

And for a long time War played cruelly with Kfar Sama, like a cat with a mouse. Some shells going off here . . . some others there . . . some scorched orchards . . . some roofs torn down . . . some arrests, unexplained and probably unexplainable . . . and, oh yes, Fear, all the keener as death seemed to approach from everywhere and nowhere at once.

As day succeeded day, the village would lose some of its fairy-tale spell. But it did not lose its soul. Its first big wound was the death of Karim, a young boy of barely fifteen years; Karim, whose dream it was to become a farmer and to learn how to read the winds and the clouds, and perhaps—some day—to make the grand tour of the world. . . . In his head he had a hundred thousand landscapes, and people of all colors.

In his heart he had his faith, his village with all its tenderness, the music of flutes and the *zajal*.

O NE DAY, THEN, Kfar Sama received its first shell. It fell in the orchards overlooking Aïn el-Farah, at the hour when the women were filling their jars.

Karim had stayed back gathering almonds, and Mariam, his mother, seeing him from the well, made signs to him with her *mendil*,[1] full of the feeling of amazement and gratitude that always came over her at the sight of her children.

One second later. . . .

With Karim's death it was death-by-war that threw the village into mourning: brutal, imcomprehensible, unacceptable.

Up to that point, and in spite of the noisy two-note lamentations provided at wakes by the weepers and accompanied by great gestures of sorrow, the deaths at Kfar Sama had never frightened the children. At Kfar Sama neither life nor death were hidden from them. Fadi and Joumana, Karim's younger brother and sister, remembered without uneasiness their *Téta*,[2] who had passed away when they were very small. She seemed to be sleeping peacefully, and she didn't even have any more wrinkles. Hanna, their father, explained to them that her soul was light

[1] Oriental scarf with pierced borders and often decorated with tiny multi-colored glass pearls.
[2] Grandmother.

and at rest because she had loved much on earth, because she had helped and cared for many people and had never done harm to anyone.

Every evening the family prayed for Téta, or invoked her as a saint. _Jeddo_[3] held she had worked miracles. When his grandchildren asked him what kind of miracles, he answered that, to be sure, Téta had not changed water into wine, but that she had succeeded in changing a few stones into hearts.

Fadi and Joumana were still too small to understand, but Karim laughed when he remembered his Téta getting angry when Jeddo advised her to rest for a bit. "I have all eternity for that, my good man!" she would exclaim, proudly looking him up and down. "Why do you want to deprive me of the joys of my old age?"

At Karim's death, Jeddo shrank all at once. He took up speaking to himself in the house and on the road. He did not talk drivel; far from it. But he called all boys "Karim" and would welcome them with touching joy.

Joumana would spend hours with him. She didn't dare go outside the house much. After the first bomb there were others . . . many others. One was never sure of when they might come down. Until now they had fallen in woods and orchards. One day they could just as well crash down on the houses. And then. . . .

Joumana would sit next to Jeddo and put her head on his knees. Mariam had asked her to look after him as much as her little heart was able. She had also asked her to look after Fadi, who seemed so remote from everything. Joumana would go from one to the other, her heart full of love and her eyes full of

[3] Grandfather.

Why do you want to deprive me of the joys of my old age?

sadness. She would put her head on Jeddo's knees and listen to his monologues. She would put her head on Fadi's shoulder and listen to his silences punctuated with strange utterances. But in her distress Mama's arms were always there in the evening, and her grateful glances during the day. And her prayers never called the love of God into doubt.

S OMEWHERE IN KFAR SAMA a rooster crowed.

Jeddo awoke immediately and prayed: "Blessed are you, O God, for this new day. May we, with your help, live through it in goodness, beauty and peace. *Amin!*"

Somewhere in Kfar Sama another rooster crowed.

Jeddo loved this primitive and triumphant cry in the silence of the dawns of the mountains. It proclaimed a mysterious assurance and, at the same time, an invitation to greet the rebirth of the day. Jeddo got up, slipped on his brown leather babouches, put on his shirt, whitened by laundress's blue, and his black *sherwal*,[4] held at the waist by a long, broad belt which on occasion served as a pocket. He clung to these old-style clothes, so practical for work in the fields.

In the house it was still dark. Everyone was asleep, except for Mariam. She had no doubt already ground the morning coffee and stoked the coals in the kitchen stove.

Mariam!

Earlier on, her lively mirth used to delight Jeddo. Mariam was happy to be alive; happy over her husband and her four children; happy with her *mendils* incrusted with tiny pearls and with her sachets of lavender, which she slipped in between the piles of white sheets.

---

[4] Puffy Arabian trousers tightened from the calves to the ankles as shown in cover photo.

Through and through, Mariam was a mountain girl, well rounded, fresh and firm like an apple from the Sannin.[5] Jeddo blessed Heaven and his son Hanna for having given him such a daughter-in-law. Although less stormy than Téta, Mariam nonetheless had the same trait of tenderness and that exuberant manner of speaking which can lull a child's sleepiness or sorrow: a singing language that ignores syntax and uses words that are no longer words but bubbles of tenderness, reaching a person's deepest parts without going through the intellect; bubbles of love that are as precious as mother's milk.

Jeddo remembered with nostalgia that Téta walked straight and firm but never overwhelmed anyone. She would always speak her mind, and give you the quick, tangy answers of the country-women of old times; but she also had the exquisite delicacy of simple people, which you would look for in vain in handbooks of etiquette. Jeddo thought that life near Téta had been sweet and good. She had borne him four boys and two girls in the course of life's usual aches, without any complications or unnecessary complaints. With remarkable equity and spiritedness she had distributed a few ounces of punishment and tons of caresses. And her little brood throve very well under this regime!

Later on, mellowed by time, she had become a veritable Christmas tree to the big children scattered throughout the village, and to her own grandchildren she tasted like the honey that was reserved for feastdays.

Every new birth in the family excited her as if it were the first. She would announce it like some extraordinary marvel, and invariably she would exclaim: "It's a boy, and handsome as his father!" or "It's a girl, and beautiful as her mother!" And

5 A mountain in the chain of Mount Lebanon.

cupping her hands about her mouth she would shout to the four winds the traditional modulated cries of joy.

Yes, indeed! Life continued in spite of death, and memories warmed old hearts.

Memories?

Formerly Mariam would greet Jeddo with a joyous: "Fair morning to you, father-in-law!" And she would hand him a cup of steaming coffee, saying: "May you drink it in good health and happiness!" And Jeddo would answer her with an enthusiastic: "Fair morning to you, my daughter. May God prolong your life and your children's!"

Formerly, when Jeddo cursed war and bemoaned a lost future, Mariam would gently shake him and say: "Come on, father-in-law! Don't put stains on the day before it's finished! We need every bit of our faith. Let's not weaken it by complaining."

Formerly . . . that was the spring of the previous year. Since then the summer had lost its sun and the day had indeed come to an end.

The day: which is to say hope, courage, the ability to feel life in and about oneself, and to love it.

Formerly . . . that was before Karim's death. Before the insane deaths of thousands of children in a land sweeter than the breath of the zephyr.

"Karim, light of my heart," Jeddo whispered, "may the light that has no end shine for you! Téta died, as did many of our dear ones. May God be merciful to them! This was great sorrow to me, but their passing away was somehow in the order of things. Téta passed away in peace, because the oil in her lamp had run out and she had accomplished with faith and trust her task on earth. And this somehow seemed right. Very, very sad, but right. For me also the oil is running out. The earth awaits me and Heaven—may it forgive me my failures and my weaknesses! I shall sleep in the good earth of our village, in the fragrance of mint and of thyme, and this too will be in the order of life.

"But you, eye of my soul! Was it in the order of life that you should be killed? Is war in the order of life? Is it the will of Heaven?

"No, my child! God no more wants us to kill than He wants us to take our own life. On the night of the Nativity the angels sang: 'Peace on earth to men of good will.' Peace, my child, is love and justice. A just man is full of love, otherwise he could not be just.

"No, light of my home! War is not the work of Heaven. It is the work of man consumed by ambition. You know our saying: 'Don't let ambition enslave you when God has created you free.' Ambition minces up men and lands. It goes out hunting for men's lives. It is deaf to the cries of the wounded. And cries of pain turn into cries of vengeance. And vengeance, in turn, brandishes the flag of violence. In the name of justice and human rights. . . .

"And there's never an end to war.

"I'm nothing but an old man, my child, ignorant and simple. But I know that the rights of man are found in the Lord's Commandments:

" 'Thou shalt love thy God, and thy neighbor as thyself. . . . Thou shalt not kill. . . . Thou shalt not steal. . . .' "

"Are these commandments from another age? We, tillers of the soil, we see in them true justice and true respect for the rights of every man:

42

"Not only shall you not raise a hand against another's life, either in words or in deeds, but you shall do everything in your power to protect life and to contribute to its fruitfulness.

"Indifference, like hatred, is heavy with darkness.

"Not only shall you not steal, but you shall be attentive to the needs of those who are weaker and more bereft than you.

"Selfishness, like theft, strips your brother bare.

"Are these ideas irreconcilable with man's intelligence? Is war the inevitable road for the triumph of man's rights?"

"Listen to the rooster's crow, you who are the song of our hope! Listen to the day that is coming from beyond the mountains. Your mother awaits me for the morning coffee. We don't speak about you. Not yet! Both she and I speak to you in the sanctuary of our hearts. And your father too, no doubt. Because if we believe in the presence of God, we also believe in yours. You are here, with us. The big stove in the kitchen purrs on as usual, and in the bowls that you used as a child the whiteness of the *labneh*[6] is dazzling among the bunches of mint and the gold of the olive oil.

"Oh, this smell of undershrubs and happy childhood! What a sweet gift, so good and so easy to share. Are these only the poor joys of poor people?

"Karim, since you now see and know everything, tell me what happiness, what kind of balance can men find in violence?"

[6] White, creamy cheese.

43

The horizon is red and the city is black.
Tomorrow there will be good weather over a torn country.

NIGHT IS FALLING, my child, and the horizon is red. Tomorrow we'll have good weather.

"The horizon is red and the City is black. Tomorrow there will be good weather over a torn country.

"Do you hear the thunder of the shells? More of this savage fury that no paroxysm breaks.

"You used to ask: 'Jeddo, why is war here? Why is there war anywhere? Can no one stop it?'

"Why war, you ask, O cedar of my garden? I don't know. I don't understand. In Kfar Sama politics does not impassion people. In his Sunday sermon *Abouna*[7] said: 'The children of Biafra are dying of hunger. What can we do, since our earth yields so many good things? What can we do, we who love our children so?'

"He went on:

" 'I was hungry and you gave Me to eat. I was naked and you clothed Me.' "

"Before this we had never even heard of Biafra. But we knew that a child's suffering is the same in all five continents. His hunger is no less awful if he is black or amber-colored; his cries are no less piercing if he is not our child.

---

[7] "Father", referring to a priest.

45

"And our wives would say: 'Husband, you know the saying: "If you're unjust to an orphan you're unjust to your own children." We have two big sacks of *bourghoul*[8] for this season. Our children—*in'shallah*[9] they may bury us—don't need that much. We could sell one of our sacks and send the proceeds to the little ones overseas.'

"And we husbands answered: 'You know, wife, the managing of food supplies is not the affair of the men. Give what you want! Give according to your heart and not following your reason. Reason's figurings are always full of mistakes. If your neighbor has to step out, even for a moment, and she leaves you her newborn baby, you're not going to let him cry while you rock your own! You'll nurse both babies at once. And she would do the same, of course. Has either of you ever weighed the milk you've given out like this? Falling short of your milk, then, give your *bourghoul* and some flour, too. Go on! God sends things through the generosity of men's hearts.'

"This is how things went when we were faced with others' misery. And now it is our children who die. For whom? Why? Why the death of so many children on earth?

"Tell me, my light, tell me what are the victories of War? What is it these triumphs defend that peace itself could not safeguard?"

[8] Crushed wheat that has been pre-cooked and dried in the sun.
[9] May God will . . .

KARIM, MY CHILD, look at your friends. They bring you flowers. They often come by, and Mariam receives them as if they were you. They place flowers by your picture and pray a moment near you. They tell you how present you are among us. They too ask: 'Why war here?' I answer them as I did you, that I don't know.

"I tell them that we are not a warring people. Our history contains no famous conquests to boast of. What our history tells us is that wars always have fallen upon us from the outside. Throughout the centuries, how many waves of invaders have been deployed over our land? The fingers of my two hands are not enough to count them. The important thing is that our country has always defended itself with faith and courage, and that no one has ever succeeded in enslaving our hearts. No one has ever succeeded in undermining our love of peace. Just consider: we have no obligatory military service in our country.

"How could we love war under such a mild sky? Look at our mountains, ochre and green in the sun, mauve and blue at sunset. To look at them is in itself a prayer. They fill us with devotion and the desire to give the best part of ourselves.

"Look at our springs. In every season they modulate their singing up toward the infinite sky. They tell us that love is inexhaustible and that, like them, it has neither beginning nor end.

"Look at the sea, so close and so distant. It runs off with our dreams and mirrors the absolute in our souls. It tells us that the horizon is not a barrier but a limitless possibility for going

47

beyond the senses. It tells us that it is a good and fine thing to make progress in knowledge and wonderful discoveries and inventions, as long as we don't use any of it for purposes of destruction.

"No, we are not a belligerent people. Our hearts are not fired up by the sound of military marches. They're enthralled by the sound of the *nay* and the poetry in the least of our flowers. Our folklore celebrates the earth, the harvests, love that lasts forever, and the emigrant's nostalgia. Do you remember the "Emigrant's Song"?

> *Our village has a halo of light*
> *and is scattered over the crest of a hill.*
> *Its entrance is a stairway of flowers.*
> *On the landings on one side and the other*
> *you see roses and pansies.*
>
> *Our village smiles when you make your appearance,*
> *and the nightingale sings in harmony*
> *with the waterfalls in the woods.*
>
> *O sea,*
> *carry my greetings to my grandfather's house*
> *and to the mulberry tree in our garden.*
> *Tell them the pain of my exile.*
>
> *Carry my greetings to all the people of the village,*
> *and see whether the days of yesteryear*
> *have forgotten me or still remember me.*
>
> *Do you think our village priest has left*
> *or is he still in the neighborhood?*
> *Do you think he still*
> *passes by our house of an evening*
> *and mentions my name?*

Do you think the titmice
still peck away at our fig tree,
and that the swallows still make their nests
in the gable under our roof?

Ah, how beautiful life is in our village!

"Yes, life was beautiful in our village. And how beautiful our land is, decked out with poetry. Its flanks bear no oil or ores of any sort, the kind of riches men lose their heads over. Its flanks bear fruits and flowers in abundance. Whom could this land make envious, apart from poets and dreamers? And these do not make war.

"Our ancestors invented, not gunpowder, but a process to get crimson from mollusks. They invented the alphabet and not instruments of torture. Fascinated by the open sea, they built ships smoother than eels and captured the secrets of the winds and the stars. The polar star used to be called the 'Phoenician Star'. When one is busy questioning the stars and moving toward the horizon, one scarcely has a thought left for building fortresses and ramparts. From one end of our country to the other, no fortified walls ever interfered with the wind from the open sea. No fences ever separated your property from your neighbor's. The fortifications adorned with loopholes were the refuge of our invaders. This was the first thing they always rushed to build in our land.

"In our country it mattered little where you came from. Both the friend and the stranger were equally called 'brother'. 'May God be with you, brother!' This is how we say good morning. 'May God bring you back in peace, brother!' This is how we say

49

goodbye. 'May God go with you and keep you, brother!' This is how we wish someone well.

"And in God we all believe. Faith in Him pervades our whole lives. Tell me then, little dove of my house, how did they succeed in arming the children of our country? How did they succeed in scattering hatred throughout such a beautiful country as ours?"

DO YOU HEAR THE BELLS, little child of mine? It's Sunday, the day of the Lord. The day of rest and recollection.

"Do you hear the bells—and the thunder of the explosions? Do you hear the fear and the sobs of your country's children?

"Their eyes are filled with fright. Their eyes are the shame of men.

"Do you hear the bells? Formerly the children used to jostle to hang from the ropes. The boys would get a start by jumping from the big white rock, polished smooth by generations of bell-ringers, and would pull the ropes and swing up, again, and again, and again . . . and we would look on, our old hearts full of joy.

"The bells still ring, in spite of the war. And those that have emigrated hear them in their dreams. In spite of the war, they still sing: 'The village smiles when you appear, and the bells celebrate your arrival. The people run out to meet you and say: "*Márhaba!* Welcome to the land of your fathers. Welcome to all the houses." '

"Here everyone is welcome and no one is alone. It's impossible to be alone when the houses are always open.

"One cannot want war when the houses are always open.

"One cannot leave a child alone in the dark when the houses are always open.

51

"If there is feasting or mourning in any given house, there is feasting or mourning for all the village people. Each one brings his heart along with a special dish, and stools, and benches and mats, or logs, and jugs full of oil or melted butter.

"Here no one is alone. Here children have a hundred fathers and a hundred mothers, and even more *jeddos* and *tétas*. Here, when it's cold, they fall asleep near the stove in the winter room, on woolen mats where the fire's warm reflections dance.

"They fall asleep with heads leaning on the knees of their mothers and sisters, or of their 'aunts', which is to say all the neighbor-women. And the weight of their heads is a blessing from Heaven. They fall asleep lulled by the crackling of the logs, the soft purring of the coffee pot that boils continually, the scent of the orange peelings that are mingled with the embers, and the familiar voices of the evening visitors.

"Here the evening is the privileged hour when time comes to a halt at Kfar Sama. The village people pass from one house to the other without knocking at the door. With their hand they touch first their forehead and then their heart and say: 'A fair evening, neighbors! *Shta'na* . . . we felt a longing to see you.'

"When the weather is good, everyone sits under the trees. The children fall asleep right on the pungent grass, and the evening breeze plays in their hair.

"Here people don't say to one another: 'Come by the house one of these days.' They say: 'Come sit down. Come take your place in your house.' Because here everyone knows that 'the smallest dwelling holds a thousand friends' ".

⚜

"What, then, has War come to do here? No one wants it. No one would say to War: '*Ahlan wa sahlan*. . . . Be welcome to your home.'

"Tell me, then, little child of mine, what evil spirit showed War the way to the peaceful shores of our gentle Lebanon?"

D O YOU HEAR DEATH'S thunder, O dove of my house? For hours now it's been rolling about the hills. And Kfar Sama holds its breath.

"The sea still shimmers at the foot of the mountains, but we can no longer see the coast, drowned as it is by the smoke of the conflagrations.

"When will it be our turn?

"As far as I'm concerned, I'm not afraid of death. I'm afraid of violence. I'm afraid that childhood itself might die in this inhuman world. I'm afraid for the living-dead children that will be born to tomorrow's all too powerful men."

"Today, like every Saturday, our children have taken flowers and prayer intentions to the Virgin. On the road Joumana read me hers:

" 'Holy Virgin, tell all other children how much we love them and how much we think of them, and that we send them everything we can. Tell them not to lose heart, and that we pray that Lebanon may be reunited and that everybody may love one another. *Amin.*'

"And Fadi, lost in his fear, whispered: 'Jeddo, what's the sense of all this?'

"What can we answer?

" 'Once upon a time, very far from here, an unbearable injustice was committed which led to another . . . and then to another . . . and then to another. . . ?

" 'Once upon a time there were people who, after being persecuted, themselves became persecutors . . . and so on and on . . . until the end of time. . . ?

" 'Once upon a time there was greed, and haughtiness, and intolerance, and selfishness. . . ?' "

"And yet, once upon a time there was also Love made man, and through Him we came to have Life in ourselves, now and for all eternity, a Life so beautiful, so loving, and so worthy of being loved."

"Fadi asked again: 'Since violence leads only to death, why don't they stop it?'

"The abnormal thing about this war is that the 'they' is as vague as the wind. The 'they' changes color and consistency every week, if not every day. What can I tell you, Fadi? The confusion is total. That's peculiar to wars. It's peculiar to all conflicts, whether armed or not, where yesterday's friends are today's enemies, and today's enemies are tomorrow's friends. Friends and enemies applaud or kill one another according to the direction from which their wind is blowing. And you always hear the same demands and the same protests, the same threats and the same retorts, the eternal echo of death's cymbals, the same desolation from one end of the earth to the other.

"Peace: is it with the blows of hatred and injustice that men expect to teach it to the children of the earth? Is it by means of blackmail and crime that one claims to be able to impose peace on the world?

"If it is built on hatred and the law of the strong, peace will remain at the mercy of hatred and the strong. It would be the same as building it on a volcano! Oh, Fadi, we see violence and it horrifies us. We know peace and we know it is bliss. It is the very presence of God among us. What would we be if we cannot keep this Presence at the moment when it is most necessary to us?"

⚜

"Oh, Karim! In spite of this war's confusion, we have tried to understand, we simple mountain people. We have carefully looked into newspapers and television programs. What we've come to see is today's world and the incredible jumble of poisoned values it serves up to our children. And still, on the one hand there are so many beautiful things. But on the other, what is called freedom has become an unrivalled slavery of both soul and body. This world has no use for prayers and verdant hills. Soon there won't even be any more landscapes. Nuclear bases, steel fortresses, canalized streams and thinking robots will be the sights all the countries of the earth will proudly show tourists.

" 'Jeddo, what was a "tree" like? Jeddo, what is meant by a "flower"?'

"This is what our grandchildren's children will ask them when they leaf through their storybooks.

" 'Jeddo, what was a "soul" like?'

"These things cannot be explained without the breath of love and open spaces. And Jeddo will answer with vague nostalgia:

" 'Flowers? I saw some in my youth. A soul? I also sensed one in my youth. It was . . . how can I tell you . . . ask your computer, my dear. It will give you some approximate picture. It will give you some samples of the notion of God entertained by men of former times.'

"If mankind survives, that is!

"Maybe then the incomparable tenderness of a brother's glance, the incomparable warmth of a brother's hand, the meadows studded with daisies and the waterfalls crowned with the rainbow, will spark the dreams of tomorrow's men when they endeavor to find a soul in their labyrinthine machines and in their stainless steel armors."

KARIM, LIGHT OF MY LIFE! Night is coming and I feel very weary. I feel there are only a few drops of oil left in my lamp. Even if I had more, the storm ready to break out over the village would make sure they were spilled. For me this has no importance whatever. We, the old, have had our share of life. But the others! The children! Upon what devastated tendernesses will they construct their peace?

"In spite of this, I want to tell you this evening how great is my hope. Because, notwithstanding the despair and the division, this country's hearts throb strongly for their land. They throb strongly because they have not deserted God. Because of this, no force in the world will succeed in chasing love from Lebanon's heart. And this love will give her back her strength and her unity.

"We no doubt made the mistake of living the carefree lives of people flooded by the sun.

"We no doubt made the mistake of not realizing the full measure of the misery of many of our brothers.

"It's too late now to regret and lament. But it's not too late to offer, again and again, our share of love, and to build up to the end what hatred has destroyed.

"Had we but one hour left to live, we could still reject true death, which is the pitiless and definitive absence of God from us.

"Had we but one hour left to live, we would still have the time to preserve in our children's hearts the grains of pure wheat which they will knead with the leaven of love and justice, as Christ has taught us.

"Then Lebanon will not die. She will remain this land of encounter and exchange, this country of freedom and flowers where each person will have access to all the sun's light. She will remain so for all her children and for all those who will walk her soil with respect and love.

"Had we but one hour left to live, we would continue to build a Lebanon faithful to God; a Lebanon faithful to man; a Lebanon which will be not only the land of the Song of Songs, but the land of all the songs of the earth."

Part Three

Fadi and Joumana

SUMMER NIGHTS ON THE MOUNTAINS of Lebanon come right out of fairy tales. The sky, deep and velvety like eyes full of happiness, is drenched with stars. And the familiar shadows unfurl their silence between the murmuring of the springs and the bewitching psalmody of the frogs.

The nights of yesteryear!

The houses of Kfar Sama dream in their ivy capes, drunk with the smell of the honeysuckle.

The dreams of yesteryear!

Children's laughter, those wonderful little crystal cascades, spurts out even in their sleep.

The laughter of yesteryear!

⚜

Barefoot on the warm flagstones of her room swimming in the moonlight, Joumana stopped up her ears with two angry index fingers. She no longer wanted to hear her brother's lugubrious mutterings, which always began with "Seems that. . . ." Since Karim's death, Fadi's vocabulary had completely changed. You would say he was reciting phrases from a book, carefully learned by heart:

"Seems that the world is going to end with one dreadful explosion. . . . Seems that, with nuclear arms, they'll be able to pulverize countries thousands of miles away, just by pushing one simple button. . . . Seems that robots are going to be the masters of the earth and of all the planets. . . ."

Fadi was now nothing but a well full of absurd statements. "Whether you like it or not, that's the real world", he would declare dogmatically. And it was beginning to disturb Joumana. When Karim was still there he never spoke crudely of anything whatever. Karim was a poet. He loved the earth and the music of the flutes. He would hurry through his schoolwork to go join Jeddo and Papa in the orchards. And he would say: "I want to learn to read the winds and the clouds, the dew and the routes of the bees. School doesn't even teach me how to grow one grain of wheat. I want to be a farmer!"

Joumana sniffed sadly. Karim's voice was there in the moonlight, and his laughter, so soft and reassuring. Why had he gone away so quickly?

Joumana could again see the black day when the first shell surprised Kfar Sama. Karim was gathering almonds near Aïn el-Farah.

His last time gathering.

Joumana no longer wanted to think of the horrible explosion. She wanted to remember only Mama's words the day after the tragedy, when she was shaking with sorrow and fear:

"Listen, my dove! Karim has not gone away. He is there, very much alive in your heart and in the hearts of all who love him. The earth has drunk his crimson blood, but his soul shines in the light that has no end. His love, more powerful than the fires of war, separates us from the night that is hate.

"Listen to the spring, my dove! You don't hear it because it's

64

at the other end of the village. But it has never stopped filling the jars of Kfar Sama.

"It fills them all and still always flows over, and we all know it is there. In this way we can hear it in the taste of its freshness.

"Listen to God's love! You don't hear it because it doesn't shout to knock down our doors. But it always fills the hearts that open up to its waters, like the jars at Aïn el-Farah.

"It fills them to the brim and overflows their size, and we all know it's there. In this way we can hear it in the certainty of our tenderness.

"We weep over this accursed war that kills love even in its nest. We weep over this accursed violence and the injustice of the world which bored through the hearts of children.

"And Heaven weeps with us.

"But it would be to deny our love for Karim if we were to wish death on others in turn.

"It would be killing him a second time—along with Jesus on all the crosses of the world—if we, in turn, were to cry out for vengeance.

"Always remember Abouna's prayer at the graveyard: 'Rabbi, at the Garden of Olives You could see this too. You could see Lebanon in fire and blood, You could see the innocent being massacred. You could see the black distress of those who have no voice at the councils of war, but who have the right to receive an avalanche of suffering that nothing seems able to contain. You could see the innumerable blazes that ravage the earth. And You did not refuse to drink the cup.

" 'Was this Your hope? To believe, in the very heart of

insanity, that the forces of love will triumph over the forces of evil?

" 'Rabbi, Your Truth must be done and not only uttered. Your Justice must be done and not only uttered. And so we will not break Your Covenant by harboring the desire for vengeance in the midst of our pain.

" 'Rabbi, do not let us forget Your words: "You are the salt of the earth and its light." Do not forsake us; abide always with us and make us be a most perfect image of Yourself.'

"Love, my dove: give all your heart. That's the only remedy for war, the only remedy for our tears. In the face of violence, offer peace. In the face of hatred, give forth the light of your tenderness. In the face of injustice, open out your hands. Be like the bird on the branch, free and light, always ready to fly off but given to all and welcoming all from the inner depths of your life. Be like the flowers on our mountains, wonderful with their offerings of colors."

Mama had spoken long as she rocked her little girl. And Joumana thought it was not hard to love with all one's heart. For her there was no other way of loving.

But Mama still wept often, and Jeddo spoke to himself in front of Karim's picture, which presided over the living room. How quickly life was changing all about her! And as it changed it became more and more frightening.

With teeming heart Joumana fell asleep sighing in the moonlight. She dreamed of former times, when gathering fruit did not kill children.

Y ES, LIFE CHANGES too quickly when it finds itself face to face with War. It changes too quickly when the world turns to the rhythm of factories that produce death. It changes too quickly when there is always too much to be had by too many.

Too much injustice that tramples on some and gives others the power of making human lives the playthings of their ambitions.

Too many overfed people, alongside others that drag their skeletons about with bellies swollen, ironically, by hunger.

Too many pictures of death, insolent luxury, delirious cacophonies, frenzied adventures, too many expressions of hatred and despair.

Too many books at the schools of the privileged, overstuffed with illustrations, commentaries, exercises, while the children of misery don't even have a school.

Too many alluring advertisements that day by day sink ever deeper needs into our conception of happiness.

Too much contradiction and disproportion.

Today's children live in a constant state of overexcitement, and the heroes in the comic books—the supermen, superstars, supercriminals and supergadgets—reign supreme as the masters of our children's future as adults. Without even needing to budge from their living rooms, they are daily served a generous diet of extraterrestrial monsters, electronic robots, unscrupled gangsters who happen to be millionaires, cataclysms, crimes and, above all, wars, both interplanetary and terrestrial.

In their adventure books and their television programs, the good are armed to the teeth no less than the bad. Everyone uses and abuses the same methods of intimidation. Everyone uses and abuses violence.

Violence in the raw, in a world without gravity. Violence in the midst of a din like that of an earthquake.

What countervalues do we offer them? The story of Jesus? Love, respect, honesty? All of this seems so pale to them, compared to cosmic convulsions! So pale, compared to the power of wealth and of arms!

Where is the climate of hope where the soul of today's children can blossom, caught as they are between reality and fiction?

Caught between affluence and destitution, where can they find true happiness?

Who will show them the riches of brotherhood?

Who will put in their hands the games of Life and abolish the games of Death?

JOUMANA COULD BARELY remember a time when no one spoke of war. But she could clearly remember the day when, for the first time, the dark cloud of fear blackened the invariably blue sky of her childhood. Walid, her little brother, had just been born. Inside the house, full of festive spirit, aunts and neighbor-women were helping with the long preparation of the *meghlé*[1] when Papa came in to tell them what was happening on the coast. Joumana was only four years old and didn't understand much. She was nibbling on nut crumbs while she waited for Jeddo to finish the little windmill he was making her that day. And suddenly everyone started talking at once. From that moment the transistor radios did not stop sputtering in all the houses, reporting events that became more and more un-believable, more and more hallucinatory.

Nevertheless, the disturbances were still taking place far away from the mountains, and no one believed they could last long. But not only did they not come to an end: they rather gained ground rapidly, and soon the whole country was rocking with astonishment and horror. In no time at all the face of cities and villages became ravaged. Heaps of ruins, deaths, abductions, tortures, enforced flights and famines became the daily bread of a dislocated Lebanon.

It became a wretched, interminable war, so all-pervasive, so

[1] Sweet prepared on the occasion of a birth, consisting of rice flour, cumin and powdered sugar, and heaped with pistachio nuts, pine nuts and almonds.

deeply imbedded in men's thoughts and in the very landscape that it was soon impossible even for children to think of anything else.

Joumana could no longer even imagine a future without war. She too awaited her turn to die as she saw the floods of bombs drowning the coast and a large portion of the mountains. By sheer force of hearing talk of death and seeing death, it was impossible for her to feel she was really alive.

One day, ruffling her hair, Jeddo said to her: "You, my little bird—it's still such a great joy to see *you* so alive! May God protect you from every evil!" Joumana looked at him with great big eyes. She seemed to suddenly become fully conscious of a feeling only half-perceived till then. And her reply summed up the anguish in which are immersed the children of War: "Me, Jeddo? Me, alive? I don't know. . . . Fear is all I feel." And Jeddo hugged her tightly with his old arms and wept like a little child.

For Joumana the most awful part was the nights. You couldn't see light anywhere and Kfar Sama seemed isolated between sea and sky. And too, after sunset, it seemed War doubled its fury. It relentlessly hammered at the mountains with its monstrous blows and dreams spent themselves as exhausted nightmares.

In the old days, Beirut and the mountains would light up at the same time as the stars, and all of these lights, dancing to infinity, clothed the nights in a lavish garment that glistened like paradise.

Karim would say: "You really can't tell whether it's from earth or from Heaven that these myriad jewels pour out, and they're more beautiful than all the treasures of all the sultans of the Orient. Ah! The stars and men's knowledge are two things that know no frontiers. No power in the world can subject them

70

and domineer them for its own profit alone. Why must millions of people be crushed for the profit of any one power?"

Then came the black nights with restrictions of all sorts. Only the stars shone—far, very far away, in an inaccessible firmament—and Karim no longer said anything.

Joumana knew there were refugees everywhere. On the road-sides and on the beaches, in the woods, the schools and the convents. Everywhere! Some months earlier, on Christmas Eve, Papa had taken his children to a partly demolished school on the outskirts of Beirut, to help with the distribution of some crates of apples and cakes made in the village. Joumana had come back totally bewildered. To think that this could happen to anybody at any time!

Joumana had never seen such destitution. At Kfar Sama no one was either rich or wretched. They were poor all right, but they neither suffered hunger nor trembled with cold. Although they did not have the means of gorging themselves or buying piles of fashionable trinkets and knickknacks, they did live in tidy dignity under their hospitable roofs. Their children went to school and their tiny patches of land held their promise at every season. What's more, the poor of Kfar Sama did not have that look which is heavy with ravaged memories and visions of Hell—the look of painful prayer and impotent revolt.

The destitution of the refugees plunged Joumana into a fright-ful abyss of comparisons:

Misery, in the classroom readers, consists of well-turned phrases that are analyzed into clauses—main, subordinate or relative—and there are always such beautiful color illustrations that Misery becomes even more abstract. If, in addition, you have to put the text into the present, the future or the past, you're no longer quite sure whether Misery exists, will exist or has existed.

Misery embarrasses the rich, and they speak of it with a compassion laced with scorn and spite, as if the poor were poor on purpose.

Misery, for many people, is a good conscience bought at the price of an occasional alms.

The bareness of the manger becomes the sweetness and excitement of Christmases full of angels and sheep, carols, wreaths, multicolored lights and clods of moss crowned with wheat sprouts.

"Mary swaddled Him and placed Him in a manger because there was no room for them in the inn."

Christmas! Mounds of little surprises and big kisses, cakes crammed with pistachios or with dates kneaded in rose syrup, chestnuts crackling on the stove that purrs with warmth, and the tenderness of all in houses beaming with happiness.

"Because there was no room for them in the inn."

Where, then, is there room for the homeless of a world as evolved as ours?

Where do children go who have no more parents or home?

Where do the children of the dead houses go?

Into a beautiful history book? Or into a manger with Jesus?

Who will swaddle their destitution with hands like Mary's? Who will build them a manger in the warmest nook of a loving heart?

"We all will!" answered Papa. "We all will!" answered Mama.

"We are all responsible, we who have received love as our inheritance. Just because evil exists we will not give in and say there's no more room for love. Just because we cannot help the whole world, that doesn't mean we should refuse life to even one single human being, if we're able to give it.

"If we believe in love we can make it concrete at every moment. We really can work this miracle, which is God's wonderful gift to men of good will."

IN SPITE OF EVERYTHING, hope still held its ground in this little Lebanon with such deep roots. At the least lull, stand–in masons would try to rebuild the houses. Hospitals would set up bedspace in their basements, and emergency teams worked day and night without respite. Torn down schools would again open their doors in whatever premises fortune assigned them.

To be sure, there were whole families that had been exterminated, households that had been scattered; there was enforced unemployment and the frantic search for a minimal ration of daily bread. While some children were at school, others would be on the barricades and yet many others in shelters and hospitals.

There was also the new subject children learned: the terrible science of War. They knew the names of all the weapons. Their shape, weight, mechanism and range held no more secrets for them. What's more, they could pronounce the words "terrorism", "oppression", "aggression" and "assassination" with as much ease as the names of flowers and birds.

Above all there was their immense disarray and their touching prayers.

And, in spite of it all, there was in their little hearts a little lamp of trusting love that stubbornly refused to be snuffed forever.

⚜

On Saturday evenings Joumana went to church, her little hand in Jeddo's big, reassuring hand and her ear listening for bombs. She greatly loved the sacred chant, the meetings with Abouna and all the parish activities that preceded the children's Mass.

On that particular Saturday there was only the Mass. Abouna was busy with the parents. For some hours now there had been much talk of a sizable attack on the region. The mountain villages had no shelters. In any event, there wasn't a single spot that was safe from one end of the country to the other.

The church was full and Joumana kept glancing at Fadi out of the corner of her eye. He was so distracted that she continually . . . and the unity of Lebanon.

It prayed for the unity of the whole earth and, for themselves, to have the courage to face death.

The church was full and Joumana was glancing at Fadi out of the corner of her eye. He was so distracted that she continually had to nudge him discreetly with her elbow to bring him back to reality. More and more he would pass his time with his eyes lost in the void or his nose in magazines and newspapers. He had become quiet as a mouse and docile as an automaton. His parents no longer knew what to do to get him out of his daze. One thing was sure: he was afraid.

Afraid not only of the bombs but of all the relentlessness he discovered in human rivalries. The contrast was too great between the values that pervaded the life of the village and the savage clamor of a world caught up in the cogwheels of violence. Fadi realized with terror how easy it was to kill. How easy it was to destroy. How easy it was to oppress. He was hurled into an unbearable chasm by the spectacle of mass deaths, coldly decided, organized and systematized in the name of a given people's rights. He closed his eyes in supplication:

"Why so much hatred, Rabbi, if it only leads to death? Why this rage for domination, if it only leads to death? My parents say that we're rich having You, having our soul, and so many good and beautiful things You have put in us, so many good and beautiful things we can see, feel and share all through our lives. But all we see is death. We are surrounded with death, threats of death and tools of death. As for us, we don't want to kill. But no one asks our opinion. No one asked for Karim's opinion nor for that of those who prefer peace to no matter what else on earth. Rabbi, we no longer know whether we're already dead or still alive."

Fadi was shivering and Joumana watched him from the corner of her eye. Mama had asked her to be gentle and patient with him. This wasn't always easy. But nothing really was easy, starting with the unending talk of war on everybody's lips, and the uncertainty concerning the near future, which left a funny hole in your stomach and gave you the impression of walking on shifting ground. Then, too, Mama was often crying. You could tell by her red and swollen eyes. Papa had lost his heavy laughter of before. Jeddo talked to himself, even in church. Walid followed Mama around like her little shadow, and Fadi was fading away into his twisted world, a world he would only talk about at night or when he was all alone with his sister.

Outside, the mountains resounded with not-too-distant fighting. Day and night the unbearable racket filled both sky and earth. Hatred, having started out like a locomotive, now crushed, mutilated and devoured everything that fell between its jaws.

In the church Abouna was praying, and all of Kfar Sama with him: "Rabbi, teach us how to love with the love that gives a soul."

76

Kfar Sama wept and prayed. Mama wept and prayed. Jeddo talked to himself and prayed. And Fadi vanished into his twisted world. Joumana could feel that he was even more afraid than her, and her tenderness wept and prayed even as she nudged him with the elbow to bring him back among his loved ones.

Fadi was thirteen years old, and he wanted to understand. He wanted to know why the earth had become Hell itself. And why today's children have nothing to cling to. Tossed about by contradictory values and the phantoms of a paranoid world, they jump body and soul into a frantic existence or they wall themselves up within the padded silence of an uninhabited interior planet. The characteristic of today's children is that they have been amputated from their roots. And without roots, how could they shoot up solid and pliant, fruitful and fair, toward sun and storm, breeze and shower?

Without roots, they float about, strangers to themselves and ever so fragile as they struggle to become fully grown human beings. Without roots they have no more bonds to the earth and no more bonds to Heaven.

Without roots, those human cubs are bereft of souls.

"Rabbi", Abouna implored as he looked at the children of Kfar Sama, whom he knew by heart; "Rabbi, teach us to love them with the love that gives a soul."

T HE SUNSET WAS LAVISH over the gilded sea. The first star was blinking in the sky. The air was balmy and perfumed like jasmine petals.

So much beauty about a burning Lebanon intensified Fadi's confusion. He mused: "If at least this racket could stop. If the world could explode once and for all and be done with it. Weapons . . . weapons . . . and still more weapons. . . . This must be the biggest industry in the world for there to be so many. Is there no hope that one day War will run out of ammunition, just as for months now we've run out of flour? How many thousands of tons of explosives are unloaded every day in the little ports where previously only the fishermen's boats could land? And how does it happen that the shipments of arms can come their way undisturbed, while the ships with foodstuffs and medicines don't dare come near Lebanese waters?"

What a weird race of men, who in their opulence are incapable of feeding the starving and yet can fully arm the most miserable without difficulty! Weird race, that seeks by every means to discover the secrets of human cells in order to create or prolong life at will, and at the same time does not hesitate to destroy the life of millions!

Sad and distant, Fadi's voice could be heard in the blue evening air: "Seems that there are children who scavenge in the garbage so as not to die of hunger."

78

Joumana did not answer. She tried to imagine children digging around in garbage cans and she concluded this was impossible. It was much too sad and dirty.

"Seems that there are countries where children are sold, and others where people are thrown in the sea by the boatful, because no one wants them."

This really confirmed Joumana in her unbelief. She knew that unhappy children existed, even in times of peace. But children who were sold? That made no sense at all. And she couldn't even picture bunches of people thrown into the sea. It was absurd!

"Seems that rats nibble on the ears of children who live in slums and sleep on the ground."

Joumana suddenly felt so sickened that she couldn't even protest.

"Did you hear me?" Fadi said impatiently.

Yes, she had heard. She wasn't deaf. She could hear the shelling only too well. She exclaimed:

"I hate it when you begin your stories with 'seems that'! Every time you go on to tell a hideous story. As for me, seems that I've had enough! Can't you talk of anything else?"

Fadi answered sharply: "Why should I? These are true stories, aren't they?"

Joumana had no idea. Too many awful truths existed, beginning with War. She retorted with passion: "Mama says there are also very lovely truths, and that it's those we've got to choose. I don't want to hear any more of your stories. They make me sick."

Fadi gave a long sigh of resignation: "All right, if I can't even tell you any stories. . . . Seems that in a month school's starting again."

Joumana looked at him with big, flabbergasted eyes: "What? You really think there'll be any school? I don't want to go back to school. If they have to start shoving us under the benches again every time we hear bombs somewhere, I'll just faint for the rest of my life. And no one, no one at all will be able to wake me up."

Fadi didn't want to go back to school, either. But classes had to start. School meant a near-normal situation. It meant the intensity of the war was letting up and, maybe, that it was going away forever. "Rabbi", he prayed, "please let school open again and let no one be absent from my class."

The absent were children who had been crossed out by nights of delirious rage. One fine morning they would simply not answer the roll call. A couple of days later the teacher would announce, in a silence that made you want to scream rolling on the ground, that Ramzi, Sharbel or Siham wouldn't be back anymore.

On mornings like that, Death was in the classroom. Pale and all-powerful, she smiled mockingly at the horror of the children who had been thrown into disarray by her brutal irruption. Some wept silently; others became immobile, white and brittle, like the chalk in the teacher's hand, which awaited the faltering start of a lesson that suddenly was quite senseless to them.

With an abnormally hoarse voice, the teacher would launch into his little prepared lecture, trying to keep from staring at the absent student's desk.

Oh, that desk! Suddenly it was huge and almost alive, bearing the painful mystery of the absent one. All glances converged on it, hesitant, unbelieving, begging for some denial of that unacceptable piece of news.

On such mornings Fadi wholly withdrew into himself. His ears were full of humming, and he could barely hear the teacher's sad voice. He was seized by an irresistible longing to glide into sleep, and the words "country, Heaven, angel and martyr" seemed to him to float for an instant between life and death, and in the end they formed an oppressive vault which henceforth separated dead children from living ones.

At Fadi's school there were a dozen victims, all in all a negligible number, compared to the losses claimed by other institutions. But whether it was twelve or a hundred the shock was no less intense, for it was provoked by men's violence. Fadi spent an enormous amount of time trying to chase from his mind the obsessive memory of these faces which now appeared so painfully inexpressive to him, the faces of boys he had roughhoused with into Death's very threshold, without a shadow of a premonition. For months they would haunt the classrooms, the playgrounds and his nightmares.

Why were these faces returning this evening, heavier and more present than when they were alive? They were lying on the grass in the garden, bloody and mangled like Karim under the almond trees. Like all the pictures of horribly mutilated bodies he saw every day in the newspapers.

Karim had had a horror of violence. He was a poet. He loved the earth and the music of flutes. He loved everybody. He gave as he received, with the same spontaneity and the same happy smile. Why did he have to die in that way?

81

Fadi was overwhelmed by the feeling that the weak and the unarmed were not really persons, but objects at the mercy of the goals of the more powerful. He attempted to imagine a world without possessions, without rivalries, without frontiers; a world of tenderness; a world all Kfar Sama, now and always bathed in the soft sun of his childhood; a *Kfar Allah*[2] where the most important and most precious good would be Life itself, in its grandest and humblest manifestations; a world where each human being would answer to the name of "Man" and not of "Thing". He thought of Christ crowned with thorns. "Behold the Man!" he said to himself with strange lucidness. Behold Karim and all those who only ask to be able to love and be loved. But there are no more men. There are wolves, foxes and sheep. And these cannot amount to human beings. . . .

Impersonal and monotonous, Fadi's voice was then heard in this haunted evening:

"Seems that, in some schools, they've gathered up the pieces of children with a shovel."

"Oh, no!" shouted Joumana. "You're not going to start up again?"

How he would have liked not to start up again, this small boy, so young and so anguished! But how could he think of anything else in this hellish uproar?

"Hell is now", he said. "It's the world. It's war and it's terrorism and all of those complicated words. Abouna says that Hell is where there isn't any love. We *are* in Hell, since everything is burning. Everything! Everywhere! And we ourselves are going to be burned up along with the trees and the houses and the whole world."

[2] Village of God.

"No!" screamed Joumana. "It's not true! I love everybody! Papa and Mama love everybody! Abouna and Jeddo love everybody! Karim loved everybody! You can see clearly that Hell could not be in our midst since we all love one another!"

O N THE FOLLOWING DAY Kfar Sama began paying its tribute to War. For seven days and nights it was bombarded without mercy.

On the sixth day, taking advantage of a lull, Abouna rang the church bells. And Kfar Sama—at least what remained of it—quickly came as it always had.

Kfar Sama took refuge in its church in order to pray and forgive. It was still convinced that hatred brought only hatred in its wake, and that only love and mercy could put a final stop to the slaughters of this world.

Hand in hand, Fadi and Joumana took the path that led to the church. Papa had died helping Abouna and other men from the village give first aid to the wounded. Mama, Jeddo and the little brother had been caught under the rubble of their house.

Hand in hand, the children of Kfar Sama took the paths that led to the church. They looked about them with wide-open eyes. But they could no longer recognize their village. They could no longer recognize their landscapes, only yesterday as familiar and reassuring as the purring stoves in their homes. Their accustomed paradise appeared to them strange and alien, black

Their accustomed paradise appeared black and hostile,
immobilized in the crushing desolation of an apocalyptic storm.

and hostile, immobilized in the crushing desolation of an apocalyptic storm.

"The birds aren't singing anymore", Joumana whispered. "You'd say there weren't any left."

But Fadi didn't hear her. He had no thoughts left, no tears, no reactions. His whole being had become explosions, flames, infinite fright.

In the church Joumana clung to him. Mama wasn't there to provide the rampart of her love. Hands reached out to her, but she couldn't see them. All she wanted was this brother who didn't hear her; this brother who was submerged in the vile terror imposed by men's cruelty, which tears children's lives apart and condemns them to roam in dark, echoless labyrinths; this brother whose silence was as unbearable to her as her mother's absence.

"Fadi!" she pleaded while beating his chest with her little tight fists. "Fadi, there's only us two now. Tell me we're not in Hell! I beg you to answer me. I'm so afraid and I love you so!"

And then, through the imploring call of this little girl who was offering him her fear as she had always given him everything else, through these cries that appealed to his own voice in a final effort not to sink into an endless night, Fadi realized that life was not only to be found in the apparent movements of a human body. Life, rather, was to be found in a glance which could only capture the light if another glance came to recognize it and love it.

Life meant being called out and responding to this appeal. And to respond to an appeal was to share in God's infinite love.

⚜

And this life asserted itself in Fadi in the pandemonium of the bombs that did not cease raining death on Kfar Sama. He clutched Joumana's shoulders, and his icy hands detected her tenderness with ineffable astonishment. He closed his eyes as if to hold it better and become filled with it. And then softly, very softly he put his trembling arms about her.

"Don't be afraid", he said. "You can clearly see that, with us, it can't be Hell, since we love one another."

Part Four

The Flowers of Kfar Sama

CHILDREN OF KFAR SAMA! Night is falling and you are still weeping.

O Rabbi!

How can I tell you that even the darkest nights have their dawn?

How can I speak to you of hope when, for days and days, your lives have been nothing but fright and wounds?

How can I speak to you of paradise when Hell has not yet done emptying out over Kfar Sama?

And yet, paradise is there, in the heart of your suffering, since at death's very threshold you utter a final No to hatred and you forgive.

Since at death's very threshold all I see in your eyes is prayers and love, love ever so aching but always confident and boundless.

Ever since this morning we have been gathered in our little church, with walls scarcely thicker than those of your houses. It can come crashing down at any moment and you know it. It's just that here we are all together, all huddled together very close to the tabernacle.

Very close to God's Heart.

Look at the sanctuary lamp. Its soft glow is a star within the

Our little church with walls scarcely thicker than those of your houses

darkness of the war. And you are yourselves stars, even softer and brighter, because in you your undiminished love is the most beautiful song of hope.

Ever since this morning you have been praying and forgiving. Even you, Fadi, with your pained and imploring look. I know that you are praying and forgiving. I can tell by the way you are holding Joumana with trembling arms. I can tell by the tenderness with which you continually wipe her tears and let yours fall unheeded.

Through her you have realized that love can give life in the midst of death. You are all she has left and she is all you have left. But because you love one another, each one by going beyond his own suffering, you understand that love, even when it is most deeply wounded, cannot be fully love without forgiveness. This being the case, all the tenderness of the universe belongs to you, and you belong to it.

Children of Kfar Sama! Ever since this morning we have been praying and singing: "Rabbi, You are our road through life's snares. Rabbi, You are our companion at the hour of death."

We know that this is true, since we are praying to Him who gave us His Life. And we well know that to give one's life means above all to give one's love. And this love will remain our road and our companion for as long as we refuse hatred and violence.

And now, the night will be long . . . very long. We are going to replenish the oil in the sanctuary lamp and you are all going to cling very tight to the Heart of God.

O WOUNDED CHILDREN! As I pray and watch with you, I can see you as you were once, back when your village enjoyed peace. And I weep with you.

As I look at you, Fadi, I can see Karim and all the others who are sleeping their final sleep in the ruins of your little paradise.

To remember Karim during this somber vigil is to speak of the children of Kfar Sama, both living and dead, and of all the children of the world who are walled in by distress. It is to tell them the tenderness we feel for them and to offer them bouquets of brilliant dawns to scatter their darkness.

⚜

For those who believe in the necessity of wars, Karim is nothing but an insignificant grain of sand, the replica of hundreds of thousands which have been lost in the plot of bloody epics.

For those who believe that every human face is equally precious and eternal, this grain of golden sand, like a drop of honey, awaits us along with hundreds of thousands of others, on marvelous shores where waves lined with the moon come to scatter as if on stars.

Karim had nothing of the hero about him. He did not give his life willingly: quite simply, they stole it from him without further inquiry. If they had taken the trouble to ask him, he

Very close to the heart of God

would have insisted on his right to grow up and would have refused to die in such an absurd way.

In any event, no one could take from him his right to love, and he made wide use of it in the style of Kfar Sama: without effort and without fuss.

Today he would certainly have joined you in granting forgiveness. And this very spontaneously, especially since he had never desired, at fifteen years of age, to hold a weapon between his hands—hands which already knew about sowing and reaping and about the wonder of modulating, on a reed flute, trills that were purer than the cooing of turtledoves.

Karim's story is so simple that it could be summed up like this: "He was happy, loved everybody and found violence abominable. But, like so many other victims of war, he died mowed down by a shell. And this happened so quickly that at least he had no time to suffer."

It's just that, whether astounding or ordinary, his story is marvelous quite simply because it tells of the blossoming of a life. And no one on earth has the right to bruise a life.

Karim was born one winter evening in the bright warmth of his little house, with its headdress of red tiles. Outside, the north wind was blowing to exhaustion, and the streams, swollen with rain, spilled out over the moss that lined the hollows in the rocks with an emerald green.

That winter Kfar Sama added up almost as many snowmen as inhabitants. And the snowballs, thrown by the children, whirled through the air dense as snowflakes.

In Mariam's room the old stove snored like a big sated tomcat. The house was bursting with people who had come to help or, quite simply, to see the lastborn of the village. A birth, you see, was one of the most splendid feasts that magnified the slow pace of the seasonal tasks.

Christmas, Easter, births, engagements, the return of an emigrant . . . and the bells would tumble in their little belltower and the houses would open ever more broadly to the mysteries that gave an intimation of what awaited beyond the earth, beyond death.

❦

Children of Kfar Sama! It was thus you were born, in your little houses filled to the brim with relatives and neighbors.

It was thus you were born: expected, gazed at, touched and loved by a whole village.

Each of you was the child of all.

While so many children can never open up to life because no one looks at them with the eyes of the heart, you were the children of all.

And this is a treasure equal to the treasures of paradise.

To your baptism no one invited the fairy godmother who dispenses wealth, honors, ambitions or glory; these fairies never visit the mountains. There, the sky is too pure, the air too light, the streams too close to the living spring, the hearts too open.

But in your white cotton bassinets your parents and all of Kfar Sama deposited all the tenderness in the world.

So it was that Karim, firstborn son of Hanna and Mariam,

gentle country-folk from a mountain village, received in his turn the traditional gift: all the tenderness in the world.

And his little heart was warm all his life through.

⚜

Karim grew in age but—sure sign of good health and *joie de vivre*—not always in wisdom. I mean he was far from resembling some ideal picture, which really would have worried his parents.

He was mischievous, nosy, would drive you to distraction with his questions, and was more fidgety than the wind. He drank in the sun and the rain with wide-open eyes, and he breathed in the air of the mountaintops with all the dash of a kid-goat, so sure was he of the power of the love that surrounded him and shielded him from every taint of fear.

Do your remember the magic words that the children of every Kfar Sama in Lebanon shout like a victory cry before jumping down from a mound or an orchard fence?

Mother mine, throw me!
Blessed Virgin, catch me!

And zing! off they go through the air, as delirious as if they were floating on a cloud.

What can you fear, going from one mother to another?

If you find yourself among six hundred nests, all equally yours, scattered over the wooded flank of a marvelous mountain, your soul can reach out and touch both Heaven and earth. And when someone speaks to you of children who are deprived of laughter and bright warmth, their distress appears to you unbearable.

98

And you realize that you, poor mountain children, without silver cups, mechanical toys, whipped cream or silk collars, have a lot, a very great lot to give and to receive.

Yours to receive are the wounded children of the world; they are yours to welcome into your hearts, which have known warmth from the moment they started beating.

Yours to give is that marvelous present which was deposited in your white cotton bassinets.

And tomorrow, if life is granted you, you will realize that, now and always, you will have your forgiveness and your tears to offer, your faith and your own dispossession, the memory of your celebrations and the image of Kfar Sama, which lives on in you indestructibly, the image of your parents, your brothers and sisters, alive and a thousand times blessed in you—because the love you have received is eternal.

Children of Kfar Sama, weep no more! The Heaven that bends down over your night is immense. Immense with the love of God, with the love of your parents and of those who refuse violence in order not to lose the gift of life given them at birth.

Ah, contemplate within yourselves the six hundred nests of Kfar Sama. In this night of agony, the remembrance of these little paradises is an act of thanksgiving for the peace with which they nourished our souls by teaching them to give without measure.

If life is granted you, you will rebuild them. Perhaps they will not be more beautiful, but maybe they will be warmer, if that is possible. You will put garlands of lights on all the doors and

You will rebuild them more warmly, if that is possible.

those who pass by in the night will know that it is on earth that the gates of paradise are to be found.

Oh, look at them again! They were lowly, but so much in harmony with their landscapes, so peaceful among the trees and flowers, so alien to war and every other form of violence. They brightened up the hillside as they lay there scattered haphazardly around their belltower. One went from one to the other on little paths lined with bindweed, up odd-shaped stairs and through exquisite little gardens, where the beds full of mint and parsley by no means eclipsed the climbing rosebushes and the flamboyant dahlias.

Every garden had its bower-shaped vine, its fig tree, its mulberry bush or medlar tree, under which there was permanently stationed a wooden bench spruced up by a thick woven covering with multicolored stripes. As soon as the days got warmer it was joined by stools and chairs for the *sobhiehs*[1] and evening gatherings.

The *sobhiehs*—do you remember?—couldn't care less about the tasks of the hour. All it took was a shout from someone's doorstep: "Hey, neighbors! My *rakweh*[2] is on the fire. Come on over!" Pots, wash and ironing would be dropped on the spot and everyone went over to relax a bit while gabbing to their heart's content.

As a rule the *sobhiehs* dispensed with invitations, and frequently on the paths one passed trays heaping with coffee cups, baskets full of fruit and dishes overflowing with cakes—all of it being carried from one house to another, all of it for the sheer pleasure of giving and sharing.

[1] Literally, "matinals", which is to say visits that take place very early in the morning.
[2] Coffee pot.

At the *sobhiehs* every subject was welcome: births, engagements, weddings, deaths, personalities, recipes, food supplies, husbands, children, health, little quarrels and big reconciliations, the past and the future, superstitions, premonitory dreams or just plain dreams.

One April morning the talk was of War, and the singing of the birds seemed to come from very far away, and Kfar Sama was dismayed and began reeling with fear.

❧

Children of Kfar Sama, ever since that morning you were caught up in the storm. You just couldn't understand it, what with a brilliant sun, the springtime bursting with blossoms and colors, and your bit of mountain still intact, up above the ruins that were being heaped down in the plain.

War can brush by our doors, but as long as it doesn't enter we think it's somewhere else. And fear is dissolved into foolish hope, and death surprises us as an unparalleled injustice.

And the first pictures of mangled children made you shake with fear.

Ah, how horrible was that vision to your unaccustomed eyes!

Ah, how horrible is that reality which all the tenderness in the world has not yet succeeded in erasing and which is repeated every day all over the earth in the course of all the struggles that oppose man against man!

And the children are bereft of their laughter, which becomes a shattered death-rattle.

Children with mutilated bodies!

Children with mutilated hearts!

O supermen of today! You who intend to dominate the earth, the sky, and life itself! Kfar Sama asks you:

"What is the meaning of evil to a little child?

"What is the meaning of suffering the evil that mutilates him?"

And you, little flowers of the mountains, who couldn't understand why or to what you were about to be handed over: you couldn't stop asking:

"How can we love?

"How can we love in order to put a stop to wars?"

For you a mutilated child is a searing pain that reduces love to a floating about in suspension, rendered immaterial by its impotence. And yet I so much want to instill into you my conviction by holding you close to my heart, you, children of Kfar Sama, you the living and those who have passed on, and you, the children of Kfar Sama, the children of the whole earth, man's little ones, God's little ones, the children of His tenderness: Love is there, before, during and after this suffering, and with its keen lament it applies its balm, and from its song, so pure, Life will again leap forth.

How to love?

O children, you who are on crosses all over the world! The answer is in you, whose every wound is a clamor for love.

The answer is in you, the answer is you, because you continue to pray even through your tears.

The answer is you because you know how to forgive.

CHILDREN OF KFAR SAMA, I see you weeping still. Look! The sanctuary lamp is softly glowing in the darkness, and the heavens are immense as they stoop down over your night.

You well know that Heaven is always open, for it never shuts its own doors. How could it, since it has given us its keys? It's we who shut it every time we shut our hearts.

Ah, if we would only understand that peace is already in our hands and that glory, wealth or domination are such paltry things in comparison to infinite love!

Tell me, what do we have left this night as we gaze at the tabernacle, if it isn't the truth of our souls? What is left to each man at the moment of the Great Voyage?

"Ah", Mariam used to say to Karim, "the truth of a man is not in what he possesses. And it isn't in his words, either. His truth is in the gesture of spontaneous welcome he shows to any of his brothers. That gesture is his key to Heaven."

And Karim understood these words, because his village was one permanent welcome. It exuded so many more joys than it did sorrows! In Kfar Sama, faith, as deep as it was simple, imbued every action, and prayer was all thanksgiving and praise, and knew nothing of protests and complaints.

⚜

Thus, Karim grew in age even if not always in wisdom. He was mischievous and loved to tease, but nothing in the world could get from him a selfish act. How could he be selfish when six hundred doors were open to him and he daily went past trayfuls of sweets going from one house to another, and when he was surrounded by a cloud of uncles and aunts, *jeddos* and *tétas*, cousins and near-cousins who smiled as he passed by?

How could he be selfish, when his parents never said to him:

"Son, we are poor. Therefore, keep your hand shut tight and beware that no one strips you of the little you have. Learn how to be stronger and more cunning than the others if you want to succeed in life."

Quite to the contrary, what he always heard was: "Son, give without reckoning and *Allah byeb'at*: God will provide!"

Karim—have I already told you?—was born one winter evening. He first opened his eyes on a world dressed in white. That particular winter the north wind was plucking at the clouds more than usual. The spring that followed was all the more resplendent for it. And so the springtime saw Karim babbling under the fig tree in the garden; he there discovered his first ladybug and the warm caress of the breeze, suffused with resin, mint and thyme.

The fragrance of his mountain!

His first toys were the silky tassels of his jeddos' *tarbooshes*,[3] their moustaches that quivered with laughter and which he pulled in every direction, and their shiny beads which he

---

[3] Oriental hat, red and cylindrical, with a silk tassel.

His first toys were the silky tassels of his jeddos' tarbooshes and their moustaches that quivered with laughter.

gobbled with delight, because for infants colors are as succulent as a fruit on its branch.

Later on there were windmills, marbles, whistles carved out of apricot pits, a board attached to three little wheels on which to glide down slopes at breakneck speed, flutes, *derbakés* and what have you.

In a word, nothing but very old-fashioned things!

But I'll let you in on this secret: besides these things, Karim had the thick woods and their mysteries, the church square and the town square, oodles of friends at all hours of the day; and he was much happier than the grandest of pashas.

I can still see him as a very young boy, his hair a mess, his hands sticky with glue or wearing pretty ink gloves after finishing his schoolwork. It was in this state that he would run into the sacristy with his buddies, as dishevelled as himself, their knees all scraped, their trouser pockets bulging with the amount of marbles, tops, roasted chickpeas and other ineffable treasures they would stuff into them.

And I thought how much God loved them as they were.

They would jostle with each other, with me in the middle, vying to light the coal in the censer, or to grab the songbooks which they would then pass out with big smiles to the towns-folk, who rejoiced in those beaming grins.

And I thought how much God loved them as they were.

They jostled again to put on the choirboys' cassocks, and especially (O greatest of delights!) to hold the censer and swing it with small twists of the wrist while taking their place about the altar—suddenly more solemn than pontiffs.

And I thought how much God loved them as they were.

Those who didn't serve surged into the benches next to the little ones and their parents. During Mass some would screech at the tops of their voices like a pondful of frogs, while others enchanted us with their angelic voices; sometimes they would be perfectly recollected, at other times fidgety and distracted; but they were all beautiful, all infinitely precious, all of them children at once of earth and Heaven.

And I thought how much God loved you all as you were.

Oh, what was War looking for in Kfar Sama?

After Mass, back in the sacristy, the children would again push and tug me, begging for a drop of wine. Sometimes I would pretend to forget one of them. Immediately the rest would hang from my arm and with one voice they would protest: "Abouna, he hasn't had his drop! Did you forget him, Abouna?"

And I knew that God loved you all as you were—impatient, wild, kneeling before the altar for one last prayer, then rushing out of church like a mob, hitting, pulling and shoving, but so generous, so attentive to one another.

"Abouna, he hasn't had his drop!"

Rabbi, only one drop suffices to know the taste of the best things on earth.

Rabbi, wouldn't one drop of love be enough to make known the taste of Your paradise?

CHILDREN OF KFAR SAMA! You've fallen asleep and I go on speaking to you. . . . And to speak to you is to pray aloud, wishing with all my soul that your dreams may be peaceful in spite of the nightmare that surrounds you.

❖

Only last week your parents were still working and offering a part of their harvest to the refugees.

Only last week . . . how distant that now seems!

You would bring fruit, vegetables and cakes to the parish house for the weekly distribution. And this was only a drop of water in the ocean of the miseries of War. But Kfar Sama gave this drop from all its heart, considering itself very privileged. While so many other districts lacked water and fuel and so many homeless were dying of starvation, we had a spring, plenty of wood, enough oil, starchy food, and flour to share with others.

Once a week the women tended to the baking of the bread. They worked under a shelter of wood and stone set up behind the kitchens, which protected them from the rain and the scorching sun. On wooden trays they would lay out the balls of kneaded dough which they had prepared the day before and wrapped in spotless white cloths. Then they would sit on low stools around their ovens, their hair carefully pulled back in their *mendils* and their knees covered with a square of cloth, likewise sparkling clean.

The baking of the bread

Their ovens were very simple. The indispensable element consisted of something like a little cast-iron dome, of some twenty inches in diameter, which was very wide at the base and barely bulged. On a floor of beaten earth they would pile flat stones in the shape of a semicircle, and this little structure would then be crowned by the dome. Inside these Lilliputian huts would then crackle the fire of branches and pine cones dried out in the sun.

You were crazy about "bread day". You would fill the baskets with fuel and then, sitting on your heels, you would take turns tending the fire by vigorously fanning it with straw brooms or pieces of cardboard. All the while chatting and joking, the women would each take a ball of dough, flatten it a little in their floured hands and, suddenly, they seemed literally to be doing a juggling act. Their hands fluttered about crossing and uncrossing, the right over the left and then the left over the right, slapping the dough which began extending at amazing speed. I've never quite understood how they succeeded in spreading out these balls in this way in mid-air, with no prop other than the skill of their hands. Then they would place them hatlike on the smoking domes, and the enormous pancakes would inflate and brown in the twinkling of an eye. They would then promptly remove them and immediately take up another ball of dough.

You would then fold the pancakes in four after they had cooled and would pack them into burlap sacks, not without helping yourselves from time to time to a loaf (a discard, you insisted!) which you would swallow still sizzling, thereby burning your fingers and mouth. But this burn itself had an incomparable scent which brought together all the smells of the forest.

Half the sacks would go to the refugees, and you never ran out of questions about them: "Will they have enough with these?

Are we going to be wounded, too? Are we too going to be chased out? Are we too going to die? Have we done any wrong to those who are bombing us? Why don't they love us? Would the refugees be happy if we sent them some flowers along with the bread?"

O wounded children! Maybe tomorrow, if our earthly dawn still rises for you, maybe someone will think of sending you flowers along with your bread.

ONLY LAST WEEK you still had hope, and you were ready to share bread, flowers, your houses and your parents.

Do you remember, Noor? You would tell me: "Abouna, if we squeeze together there's enough room at our house. And my parents' heart is so big that they can love twenty new children." For an eight-year-old twenty is a huge number. You would say twenty as you would have said a hundred or a thousand. And in the evening, at prayer, you would weep real tears for the orphans.

And you, Joumana. You would say: "Karim would be very happy if we gave away his bed. Three children in his bed, three children in mine, and three more in Fadi's—that would be a bunch of children who would have a bed."

But no one any longer dared to come seeking shelter around here. The vise of the war was tightening around the mountains, and the villages were falling one after the other.

Nevertheless you were all still going to school until last year. No, no, not at Kfar Sama, which was too poor and too insignificant and which didn't even have a police station, but at Deir el-Ouyoun (Convent of the Springs), a little further down the mountainside. You would go there through woods and orchards, the older ones holding the little ones by the hand, dragging your feet as you went and galloping when you returned home.

114

Obviously, you did not like school. In the village you learned so many things that were thrilling in such a different way. Closely involved in the life of the grownups, you learned about the seasons, the winds and the flying of kites; about the rains, the tender shoots and the hoary, old trees; about sheep, goats, chickens, birds and caterpillars; about the preparing and storing of figs, thyme and raisins, which you would put out to dry on big trays of braided wicker; about wild plants and their healing properties; about the swarming life of the underbrush and, above all, about respect for your neighbor and for the earth.

No, indeed, you didn't much like school. I would even say not at all! And the finest recess yard couldn't have competed with the Kfar Sama town square.

Do you remember this "square"? It was, in fact, neither round nor square, but it did follow convention in opening out in the center of the village. To the right—or was it the left?—there were, in wavy succession, the haberdashery, the smithy and the carpenter's shop. To the left—or was it the right?—you had the pharmacy, the grocer's shop and the hardware store, still in undulation. Other shops, with uncertain names, could be found here and there in surprising nooks and crannies, until they disappeared at the edge of the main road, which was shaded by poplars. In actual fact all these little shops offered an amazing supply of ill-assorted things, something which disturbed neither the sellers nor their customers. At the pharmacists's you could find marbles and newspapers; at the hardware store starchy foods and cakes; and at the grocer's both brooms and aspirin.

Under the arched porches, well-worn rickety tables and chairs patiently waited for the evening's activities. At about six o'clock, the workday now over, the men would start arriving in little groups, freshly shaven and wearing shirts whiter than snow.

115

Under the arched porches

After exchanging the usual greetings, they would install themselves without hurry and begin smoking a *narghileh*;[4] or they would fight it out over the backgammon board; or they would simply sip their coffee or finger their beads while chatting quietly. Under their indulgent gaze the children played, ran, and whirled about while screeching with delight, and the young men and women harmonized their strolling and discussing with the wonderful spontaneity of the evening breeze.

Do you remember the celebrations on this gritty square? From one poplar to another the men would crisscross garlands hung with the little lamps that you yourselves made.

I can still see you sitting on the floor in the parish house, surrounded by jars of white glue and rolls of crepe paper. You would first cut out long strips in blue, red, green, pink, yellow and white. You would then unfold them with your fingertips, your noses wrinkled, your tongues slightly showing, and for a little while you would be as quiet as mice.

Ah, you were quick of hand and quick of leg! Next you would start running from one house to another, transporting seats, baskets of fruit, bowls of olives and jugs of syrup. Your parents let you take care of the shopping. Boisterous as you were, you were also respectful, and you would return with full arms saying: "*Jeddo, ammo*,[5] *emmé*:[6] there! I didn't forget anything!"

Sometimes, of course, you would break something. You would then offer your excuses full of contrition, alleging, like all the children of the world, that you hadn't done it on purpose. And your parents would exclaim: "Honey on your heart! You didn't get hurt, did you? *In'shallah* you may bury us!" Which

[4] Oriental tobacco pipe that passes its smoke through water.
[5] Uncle.
[6] Mother.

means: "May it be God's will that your life extend far beyond ours." And also: "We love you so much that your life is much more important to us than our own." It was only when they were assured of your safety that they thought of examining the damage done.

Do you remember the wedding celebrations? You would run out of the bride's house, where the women were admiring the modest trousseau and seeing to the final details, and hurry over to that of the bridegroom, where the men were rolling their cigarettes all the while blurting out the customary good wishes, sayings and jokes. Under the pretext of helping to pass out the sweets, you would taste everything and fill your pockets with rice to throw at the newlyweds when they came out of church.

And the processions? For that you were as perfect as angels, all dressed in white, finer and more fragrant than the incense and the gorgeous bouquets of flowers that you would lay at the feet of the Virgin. On such days your souls were transparent, clearer and deeper than a pond in the summer. You, children of the earth, tabernacles of God's face, which dwelt in the glorious mystery of your smiles: Heaven itself held its breath when it saw you go by.

With the coming of War the celebrations took to flight. Those were considered fortunate who still had their homes, their work and their hope:

The hope that the world would shake off its lethargy in the face of so many horrors. The hope that it would understand that all wars do is destroy and that, soon, no one would be able to escape. The hope that it would realize that life, every life, is made to open out to love, justice, peace, and that it is murderous to turn life away from this end or to sap the promises it has of arriving at its goal.

Men do not come into the world for the sake of wars, oppression, machines, the sovereign and dehumanizing progress of technology, the establishment of one's ascendancy and renown over others. They do not come into the world for the sake of the world. God created the world in order to make their souls blossom through their human condition. He created it with His love. And He has left us this love as our inheritance, which we can acquire and scatter abroad without money, weapons, curtsies, flatteries, ruses, verbiage . . . and which has no need of petroleum, factories, machines and assembly-line slavery in order to assume the fairest forms and invade all the markets of the world.

Love! This is the world's thirst, this the sap of life, this the treasure most flouted by man.

"Rabbi, what must I do to have life?"

It is strange that God's first commandment is not addressed to reason. It is strange that it doesn't say: "Acquire wisdom and you will reap its fruit. Be attentive to your brothers and to the goods I have entrusted you with and you will be rewarded. Avoid evil, because it would bring you suffering. . . ."

His first commandment is addressed to the heart: "Love! Love thy God and thy neighbor and thou wilt have life!" He commands us to love as if He wanted to coerce us to be happy. Love! and all the rest will come to you besides: peace, justice, serenity, restraint, generosity, sensitivity to the marvels of creatures and creation. Love! and you will be astounded by the lightness of your soul and by the splendor you will see in a child's most fleeting smile.

CHILDREN OF KFAR SAMA! You sleep nestled under the altar, and I think of your brothers and sisters that are sleeping their final sleep in the ruins of your little paradise.

I see them right at your sides, Fadi, Joumana, Noor . . . and you too, little Imad, who are desperately sucking your thumb and calling out for your mother. There is a woman coming to you. She takes you in her arms to feed you the milk that her own child won't be drinking.

"Woman, behold your son! He is yours, since you are giving him life by giving him your milk. He is doubly yours, since you are giving him your love in the midst of your own immense suffering."

Woman, do you remember the wonderful stories we've been told all during this war? Do you remember that old man among the refugees we were trying to help? He told us that one night, during heavy bombing, he found himself in a shelter with people mostly unknown to him, and a little girl came to put her blanket around his shoulders. Without saying a word she smiled at him and went back to her parents. But he couldn't accept keeping warm while she shivered. And so he said: "Take back your blanket, little angel, and may God give you long, happy days, because you've transported me to paradise." But the little girl's father answered:

"Keep it, *jeddo*! If it's true that in paradise everything is given away, it's also true that everything there is received."

And, like all the others, this little girl had nothing of the heroine about her.

Who would look for a great feat in her gesture? Or for courage above the ordinary? Like all the rest, she too was trembling with fear. Nevertheless, she gave a token of absolute generosity: not out of her abundance, but out of her destitution.

You, woman, have nothing left but your milk. And you are giving it away while your whole being is clamoring for your lost child. All the little girl had was her blanket. She gave it away to a stranger who had even less.

Woman, a gesture of love is enough to transform a shelter into paradise.

A gesture of love is enough to transform the greatest pain into hope.

THE DAWN IS STILL DISTANT and the fighting is doubling in violence. Imad has fallen asleep in the arms of his new mother, and he smiles in his sleep. In Kfar Sama no child will remain an orphan. Every woman of this village will take care of him like his own mother. Every man will nurture him like his own father.

Oh, why War here? Why War anywhere?

That morning Karim again asked himself this question, one too many times, this accursed question which ought never as much as graze a child's lips.

The day before, Deir el-Ouyoun, the lovely village with nine springs down the mountain from Kfar Sama, had been massacred without apparent reason and without warning. It had been a peaceful village where people of different religions lived on good terms with one another. Those who got away had taken refuge in Kfar Sama, and Karim learned of the death of Haitham, his friend. They had met in their first year of school. They quickly became inseparable, sharing the same love of nature, the same aversion to too violent games and, later on, the same passion for poetry and music.

If he took a shortcut through the woods and the orchards, Karim could make it to Haitham's house in less than fifteen minutes. From there they would go to school together, as gentle and trusting as the sparrows that populated their gardens. In ten years their friendship had had ample time to blossom, down to the silences between them which, like a breathlessly held chord on the organ, displayed as in a rainbow the deep vibrations of their perfect attunement to one another. The simple matter was that both of them remained poets in that childlike way which found fascination in the song and shimmer of water flowing from a spring, which could endlessly play with a single ray of sun. They could both become drunk on the music of flutes, and they intuitively knew that it had been created for the mountains just as organs had been made for cathedrals.

The only thing was, you see, that they didn't belong to the same religion. That this could introduce a dissonance into their friendship was something that totally escaped them; but such a difference delighted the very heart of War, which was always tracking down the most minute shades of disagreement so as to feed its own flames.

That particular morning Karim was supposed to work in the orchards which overlooked Aïn el-Farah and which were terraced in semicircles up to the top of the hill. Beyond, an ocean of pine trees covered the mountains, descended following the gentle slopes of the terrain, and encircled a multitude of other little villages and other little orchards, before yielding to the orange, lemon and banana groves of the coastline. As a rule, Karim never tired of admiring this dreamlike landscape, and he worked with abandon, convinced that his labor contributed to keeping his perceptions sharp and his spirit serene. The more he grew, the more he loved the land. It seemed to him that, by touching it with attentive hands, he took hold of a message coming from the depths of the ages, coming from that earthly

An ocean of pine trees covered the mountains.

paradise where man lived out his joy in God, still clothed in the new splendor of His creation.

But on that morning Karim no longer saw his landscapes and the land appeared mute to him. There, under the almond trees, among the daisies and the mauve anemones, he was invaded by sadness. He felt quite sad and vulnerable, quite small and lost there at the top of his hill, hurting at the death of his friend. He took his flute and played a festive tune, in order to summon back into his desolate heart memories of their childhood. But at the touch of his frozen fingers the notes quivered more mournful than a lament, and Karim mused that a song could not burgeon from the death of a child. And he wept, his face pressed against the daisies. He wept over Haitham and all the dead of this war who, although he did not know them, suddenly became familiar and dear to him, as real as the people of Deir el-Ouyoun and Kfar Sama. Each of them had a face, a name, and a glance created for the light of the earth and the vision of love, which this glance takes along into eternity.

And, again and again, Karim asked himself the accursed question which ought never as much as graze a child's lips:

Why War?

Why must it be that, in one split second, whole families should have no homes left beyond the open road?

Why must it be that, in one split second, entire houses should crumble, and that what seemed so important vanishes into smoke?

Why must it be that, in one split second, hundreds of persons should die mowed down by hatred?

Why the cutting up of Lebanon?

125

Why should the simple fact of being called "Karim" or "Haitham" overnight become a crime in itself, punishable by death?

Who gained anything by this war? Certainly not the Lebanese, who were seeing their beautiful and gentle country crumble like a sand castle, and their lives being dragged off aimlessly by the very torrents of Hell.

Karim knew that the Lebanese had not wanted this war. Their land had been requisitioned for the settling of accounts that were alien both to their history and their nature. As a preliminary no effort had been spared to divide them up into depersonalized blocks, labeled "good" or "bad" according to which side they found themselves boxed in by their religious persuasion.

For whose sake?

For what?

⚜

Karim wept, his face buried in the daisies. He could see Haitham's family, so similar to his own, simple, united, open. What was the difference between Fadwa, his friend's mother, and his own mother, Mariam? Which of the two loved more than the other, if indeed love lends itself to measuring? Which of the two tended her home with more patience, dedication, gentleness, adoration?

"Drink, my child, drink!" 'Aunt' Fadwa would say to Karim when he visited his friend. "Double health and happiness to you! My syrup is fresher than dew; and tell me, what greater joy could I have than offering it to my son's brother? You'll eat with us at noon, besides. I've made you lentils and your favorite, *fattoosh!*"[7]

"Drink, my child, drink!" 'Aunt' Mariam would say to Haitham when he visited his friend. "Double health and happiness to you! My syrup is sweeter than a moonbeam; and tell me, what greater joy could I have than offering it to my son's brother? You'll eat with us at noon, besides. I've made you *tabbouleh*[8] and your favorite, baked *kebbeh!*"[9]

The same gestures and the same words. The same heart overflowing with welcome. Yes, indeed, what *was* the difference between the two?

⚜

And what was the difference between Hanna and Qassem, their two fathers? Both of them were men of the land, men who venerated their land. Both of them lived in constant respect for every single being.

"I see you love the land", 'Uncle' Qassem would say to Karim. "Become imbued with it, because it's in the earth that you'll find Heaven's roots. It teaches you generosity when it nourishes you; beauty when it blossoms; docility when it opens out to the sun and the rain."

"I see you love the land", 'Uncle' Hanna would say to Haitham. "The closer you are to it, the closer you are to Heaven.

[7] Lebanese salad, consisting of lettuce, cucumbers, tomatoes, parsley, mint, onions and croutons.

[8] Another Lebanese salad, consisting of *bourghoul* mixed with tomatoes, mint, parsley and onions, all of it chopped very fine.

[9] Lebanese specialty consisting of meat pounded with *bourghoul* and garnished with pine nuts and fried onions.

It will tell you the reasons for the springtime and the autumn. It will tell you why darkness and why light. Why life and why death."

What difference could there be between these two men?

And Alia, Haitham's little sister, with her brown curls flowing down over her shoulders and her big black eyes, speckled with laughter: she had the same eyes and the same laughter as Joumana.

In the name of what should one of them be less precious than the other, less worthy of being loved?

KARIM COULD ALSO SEE the amber beads of both their grand-fathers, and their tarbooshes, slightly leaning to the same side of the head, and the joyful quivering of their white moustaches at the sight of their grandchildren.

Why did it have to be that, all of a sudden, Haitham's family should appear to him as more malignant than a bloodthirsty beast? Why did it have to be that, all of a sudden, Karim's family should represent a mortal danger for Haitham's?

Why did they have to become brothers who were enemies? And why did God have to be involved in schemes hatched by men?

Starting at the crib, Karim had always heard that God is love and not some general of armies, or grand arbitrator in litigations over supremacies and possessions. It had also been explained to him that peace could not be introduced by force into a heart that rejected it.

There are people like that, who die of thirst next to a spring. There are people like that, who shiver with cold in the dark because they never open up their windows to the rays of the sun. But this doesn't keep the spring from gushing its water, or the sun from illuminating and warming the earth. Springs and sun are within reach of our hearts. Love is within reach of our hearts. Peace lies in our hands. If we let it fall we have no right to make God responsible and to kill each other off in His name.

No, thought Karim. The Lebanese love their springs and the

sun, prayer and the *zajal*, too much to have wanted this war. It came from elsewhere. But, in order to force it on them, it was indispensable first to drench them, soul and body, in distrust and fear. They had to be taught that learning how to handle weapons was their only chance of survival. Afterwards Hatred could make its grand entrance by the gate of honor and crown the reigning divisiveness with one final combat with no winners. And even if certain voices should rise to condemn such hatred, what could they do against such masses in fusion which are consuming themselves and one another in apocalyptic frenzy?

⚜

Karim could see himself again as a small child, holding Haitham by the hand.

"Tell us a story, Jeddo Khalil! Tell us a story, Jeddo Hussein", they would both clamor with insistence.

"What story do you want to hear?" one or the other would answer. "I've long since exhausted my supply."

"Well, then start all over again, Jeddo Khalil! Begin from the beginning, Jeddo Hussein! Tell us the story of Si Hassan, the enchanter."

Lord, did they ever love these spellbinding stories in which the stars throbbed to the rhythm of tambourines, in which marvels would emerge like jinnees from Aladdin's lamp to prove to trusting hearts that faith can outwit obstacles and that love is the fabulous philter which alone can transform a granite mountain into a bush full of jasmine.

"*Kan ya ma kan fi haydik ezzaman.* . . . Once upon a time long ago. . . ."

O magic of these ageless stories, that can fly across time on the wings of their words! Diaphanous words, singing words, words containing huge expanses of space, words that transport children above the clouds and carry off old *jeddos* into time's endless round.

Kan ya ma kan. . . .

⚜

Stories of war are nailed to their dates and their words have a black sound, like crows perched on a gallows:

"In the year 300 . . . 600 . . . 900 . . . 1100 . . . 1975 . . . conflicting hordes tore the world apart, and the sun was extinguished for millions of men."

This kind of story has never lulled children to sleep and to dream. This kind of story shatters their dreams and their wings, and leaves them, as sole inheritance, leaden balls of darkness about their ankles, which they will drag the whole length of their unending death.

Kan ya ma kan fi haydik ezzaman. . . .

O ageless stories told by our ageless *jeddos*, stories belonging to all times and all spaces, beautiful, living stories, marvelous legends in which men communicate with the stars and the angels. . . .

O magic of life, magic of tenderness!

Once upon a time long ago there existed children who were loved.

Once upon a time in our present time there existed happy children.

In our present time once upon a time there existed tenderness, fair as the day itself, fair as the very night. . . .

There *exists* tenderness, as fair as life itself.

"O Haitham," Karim wept, "I feel your death in the deepest part of my soul. But your love will make you live again, my friend, my brother, with a life that no war can wound. We will again play the flute together under the great oak that shades the village square of Deir el-Ouyoun. We will again play it at the top of the hill, face to face with the sea and the sky, and we'll discover that the world is even greater and more beautiful than our childhood dreams imagined, because it receives the light of the sun, of the moon, of the stars. It receives it from Heaven. We will then play Heaven's melodies and our bodies will matter little.

"We will then live in a day in which evening and morning will be perpetually intermingled, because you are my brother and I am yours."

CHILDREN OF KFAR SAMA! You are still asleep, and the long-awaited dawn has just erased the stars. What will it bring us? A smile, or still more tears?

Outside, suddenly, there is silence. Strange. Oppressive. The thick silence of darkness. The silence of War, as threatening as its fits of rage. What does it conceal?

Outside, the dawn. Softly, softly, the mountains emerge from the night. Softly, very softly, their peaks become golden with the rising sun. The day begins to peek, bright as a daffodil. What will it bring us?

Outside, the sky. Blue as a child's dream. And near the altar, a bouquet of children. Marvelous little flowers abandoned in a little church. Cut off from all human support. Cut off from the world, but not from Heaven.

They awaken in the lifeless morning. Do they sense that, henceforth, all questions are useless? Do they sense that, in this gloomy silence, love is the only certitude? But even now they awaken somewhere beyond fear, and their first glance is a smile.

They no longer expect anything from a world that has savagely destroyed their gardens of tenderness. Why, then, do they smile? Is it because they know that they have everything to expect from the tenderness that comes from Heaven? Is it because they have put themselves between God's hands?

They awaken smiling, these little wounded flowers. They stretch in the rays of the sun that filter in through the sanctuary window and they say good morning to everyone. They then kneel down next to me.

And then God's Word begins making its way to the depth of their souls: "Come to me! Fear nothing! Have trust!"

And they plunge into trustfulness as only children can. They plunge in, body and soul. For them such trust as this has nothing in common with the trust men feel when everything is going well, when health is good, when one's appetite is sated, when one's friendships are gratifying, when one's purse makes a pleasant tinkle, when the future is clean of major concerns.

No! They plunge into absolute trust. Trust of the heart. Trust that insists on singing when reason has all the reasons in the world to despair. Trust that is incompatible with fear. Trust that receives everything by giving everything away, because it welcomes the immensity of Love.

"Come to Me, all of you who sorrow under your burdens, and I will give you rest!

"Come to Me and I will give you Love!"

Kneeling before the tabernacle they begin singing, these little uprooted flowers, as pure and fresh as their Wellspring of Happiness:

> *Ever since the cradle*
> *I've been nourished by Your Love,*
> *O Rabbi, and my lips*
> *will forever keep its taste.*

If the ocean is stormy I will take shelter
in the harbor of Your hands.
You are our lamp on the dark road.
You are the treasure from which we cannot part.
You are our rampart as long as dangers last,
because You are Love.
Make us come to Your wellspring and quench our thirst.

We are hungry: You are our bread.
We are thirsty: You are our wine.

Grant we may share all things
through the single bread of Your truth.
Because, if we hold out our hands to You,
we will through You be able to give all.

O Rabbi, we offer You our lives
that Your vines may be fruitful.
Grant they may never slip
from between Your hands.

On this lifeless morning they sing and pray, the little flowers of Kfar Sama. They sing and smile, like every child nourished with unmeasured tenderness. Within the dark gloom of War, at a moment when their world is no longer anything but a heap of ruins, they live on this tenderness—warm, sweet, luminous, as can only be the certainty that Love is the totality of all things, the foundation, self-transcendence and infiniteness of every human being, the paradise of profound communion with God and with men.

Whether they live on earth or in Heaven, no one can destroy

the paradise of the children of Kfar Sama—because Kfar Sama had made this paradise take root in their hearts.

Their houses with arches and a headdress of red tiles: this is their trust in God.

The enchanted waterfalls: this is their songs of faith and thanksgiving.

The flowers and the birds: this is their prayers and their sharing.

The springs: this is the love they receive as their inheritance and which they learn how to pour out from brimming hands.

The air, purer than a caliph's diamonds: this is their gaze toward God, the gaze proper to the children of God. Their forgiveness, so that Love may blossom in all its divine radiance.

That morning, when a shower of bombs broke the heavy gloomy silence, the children of Kfar Sama no longer wept.

They were now praying, pressed tight against God's Heart.

Epilogue

Eight years of war in Lebanon.

Eight long years of desolation for a tiny little country lacking all structures, pretensions, possessions and territories in the scale of such a display of violence.

For whose sake?

For what?

Why War here, and why War anywhere?

Why, in such an evolved world, must millions of refugees drag their despair about from nightmare to nightmare, their hands empty, their feet bare, their hearts hollowed out?

Why these millions of children sacrificed inhumanly to the folly of men?

O Rabbi, is it You that have abandoned us or is it the world that has deserted You?

O Rabbi, why so much hatred when tenderness can be so light?

Why hunger, thirst, fear, stench, the echoes of hellish tumult, the wailing of children, the stupor of the old, the long lament of mothers who refuse to accept the terminal silence of their little ones?

"Forgive them, for they know not what they do!"

Whom should we forgive, Rabbi, when we all have a share of

responsibility in this world which kills souls—we who have received the earth as our lot, we who have received Your Love as our inheritance?

O Rabbi, what sort of love or hatred will have kneaded the hearts of those who survive this holocaust? How to speak of love to children who have been uprooted from their gardens of tenderness to be thrown out into a night of dread? How to speak of love to all the children of the earth, who will go out to harvest fields which have been sown with poison, who have been convicted to row on galleys of fierce rivalry?

Children without a childhood!

"Let the little children come to Me!"

Let them come to tenderness, to light, to warmth, that imbued with them they may in turn themselves become tenderness, light and warmth that will radiate all around.

"Blessed are they who do a work of peace: they shall be called children of God."

A race to produce arms. A race to sell arms. A race to attain domination, possession, death.

"I give you My peace, My peace I leave you."

What peace, Rabbi, if it doesn't produce revenue? And what is one man to the majority of men? And what is the need of so many men? Machines can take their place ever so efficiently. . . . Machines know nothing of hunger, fatigue, just claims and dignity. What is the use of so many men?

But still enough of them are needed to be able to keep the arms and the illusions flowing at a profit. Enough of them are still needed to serve as exchange currency, means of blackmail, and

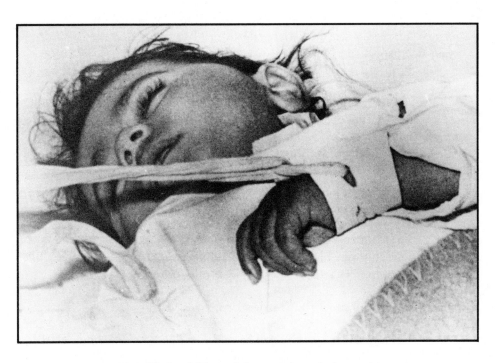

No! All the children of the earth have had enough!

guinea pigs of terror. Enough of them are still needed to go out and wage war in the name of peace, justice and human rights.

Ah, what a fine masquerade when Hatred calls itself justice and shamelessly puts on the garb of righteousness, duty and the defense of the oppressed!
No! The Lebanese have had enough!

All the peoples of the earth have had enough!
All the children of the earth have had enough!

The children of injustice . . .
The children who have been sold . . .
The children who have been prostituted . . .
The children who have been defiled . . .
The children who have been driven to suicide . . .
The children emaciated by hunger . . .
The children bloated with overabundance . . .
The children whose dawns have been ravished . . .

The children of the Garden of Olives.

They are all alike. They all have the dull look of the damned of the earth. Who will hold a hand out to them?

"We will!" shout the children of Kfar Sama. "We will!" shout all the childlike hearts of the earth. "We will hold one another's hand. We will hold hands with the whole earth. We will sing of love in the midst of the darkness. We will sing as much, and more, and much louder than hatred."

There will then be an evening, and there will be a morning. . . .

. . . And Love will once again create the world.

Baabdat, March 26, 1983

✤

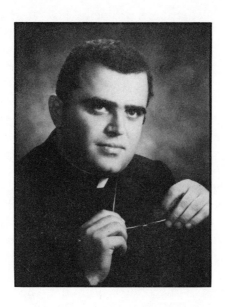

Biographical Note

Father Mansour Labaky is a Maronite priest, ordained in Beirut on March 26, 1966. He is also a poet and a composer, a promoter of Arabic spiritual songs, the director of the Christian monthly magazine *Al Rahiyyah*, editor-in-chief of the quarterly *Al Foussoul* (or "The Lebanese Seasons"), author of the hymnal *Cedars of Lebanon*, which brings together the entire heritage of the Maronite liturgy in Syriac, Arabic and English. Father Labaky has also lectured widely in the United States and in

Europe on the Lebanese problem. His writings, poems and music have been the theme of a master's thesis in Arabic literature presented to the University of Lebanon. His spiritual songs, very popular in the whole Arab world, are sung by different denominations.

In January 1976, his parish of Damour (Southern Lebanon) was massacred. He assisted at the burial of heaps of bodies of women, children and old men who had been horribly mutilated. When the hamlet had been surrounded and all outside assistance appeared impossible, Father Labaky gathered the survivors in his church and asked them to forgive and offer up their lives for peace in the world. All present responded with a song of faith and love. Against every expectation, the survivors nonetheless succeeded in escaping by sea by crowding into boats under freezing rain.

Since 1977 Father Labaky has been caring for war orphans from every area of the country. With them he formed the choral group "Little Singers of Lebanon". They may be heard singing of love, forgiveness and peace in many different places: on radio and television, at the UNESCO headquarters, in the schools. In December 1980, he held a "Recital of Hope" with three hundred fifty little singers of different denominations, and the concert had a huge impact on young people.

Having been a witness of atrocities he prefers not to dwell on, Father Labaky does not aim in this book to explain the reasons for the war in Lebanon. Imbued with his faith, and with the beauty and mildness of a country in which the names of the villages and the springs are a whole poem in themselves, he tells the story of a mountain village, similar to so many other Lebanese villages, similar to so many other villages on earth, so distant from politics and its stirrings that War remains to them forever an incomprehensible monstrosity.